HOW I
SURVIVED UNBROKEN

by

LINA LANGFORD

For information, contact: linalangford.com

ISBN: 979-8-9932445-8-7

Cover design by Lina Langford

Printed in the United States of America

Moon Light *Creations* LLC
&
Lina Langford

God, this is my thank you.

Unpolished, unfinished, but true.

Thank You for hearing the cries no one else heard.

For the dark nights and hard words when I thought I was all alone. For holding the pieces of me I couldn't hold together.

Thank You for staying with me when I didn't.

There was a season I gave up on you. I was too tired to pray, too angry to trust, and too broken to hope.

But even when I let go of You, **You did not let go of me.**

When my faith fell apart, Yours did not. When I walked away, You walked beside me.

And thank You for the greater blessings that rebuilt my life:

My husband, who stands by me tirelessly,

who loves me on the days I feel unlovable,

who calms my storms with patience and reflects Your love in the small things, day after day.

And my children, the answer to the prayers of a little girl who once drew a house in the dirt and begged You for a family of her own.

They are my joy, my healing, my proof that cycles can end with me.

They are the promise I keep every single day.

You did not erase my past, but You refused to let it be the ending.

You taught me to build a home in the broken pieces, to set a table where love is not a debt,

to speak blessings where I once heard only blame.

Now I place these pages at your feet.

Use them to lift all the heads that hang low and whisper to anyone who needs to hear it:

You can make a different ending.

I gave up on You once but You never gave up on me.

For that and everything I can't find words for;

Thank You.

To my children

You are my proof that the cycle ends here.

You are the reason *love* in our home overflows,

not wreck, not silence, not curses.

If in my human weakness I have ever failed you, please know every step, every choice, every breath was my fight to give you the life I never had.

And if I ever fell short or made mistakes,

I pray you find forgiveness in your hearts.

To my husband

The solid ground beneath my feet,

the shelter I never thought I would find.

You stood with me when I was the hardest to stand beside.

You saw me when I was drowning in shadows and called me back into the light.

You didn't just hold me in your arms, you held my story, my scars, my broken pieces, and you never let them scare you away.

Your love is the clearest proof to me that God answers prayers, even the ones whispered by a little girl who only wanted a safe place to belong.

I Love you all with all my heart!

How I
Survived Unbroken

Introduction

I'm not writing this book because I've got it all figured out. I'm not here to coach you with brilliant advice or polished lessons.

I'm here to tell you, vulnerably and openly, that I'm simply sharing my story.

Maybe as you read it, you'll find a piece of your own. Maybe you will see something that shifts your perspective, maybe you will realize you're not alone. And honestly? Maybe you will even help me, too. In the end we're all walking through this life and learning as we go.

I haven't figured everything out. There's only one person in my life who *claims* to know everything — my mother.

And if you've ever thought you were the only one struggling, I have news for you: you're not. There are millions of us. Each one carrying different battles, different wounds, different patterns.

And here's the thing about struggle, from the outside, someone else's pain might look small compared to your own. But that's not how it works. Because when you're inside it, when the struggle has built itself into your body, your nervous system, your patterns, it feels impossible to break free.

Your mindset might whisper, "You can do it. You've got this," But the toxic relationships, the voices you keep around you, the weight of those patterns...paralyzes you. And sometimes you don't even know it's happening.

I know the second I said that it stirred something in you. Maybe it makes you mad. Maybe you feel that lump in your chest, that tightness in your throat and you just want to slam the door and walk away. I get it. I've been there.

I still go there sometimes. But now I know how to step back out. I know how to catch myself when I slip back into old patterns.

Believe me, I've spent my entire life trying to figure it out but here's the truth: we can't fix other people. We can't fix the world's perception. That's never going to change. But there is one thing we can change - ourselves.

I could've written this book 20 years ago and I tried. For two decades, I wrote little pieces, and then lost track. But now I know, the time just wasn't right then.

Now I am ready.

I used to think: Who would ever care about my story?

Why would anyone want to read this?

But you're here. You picked up this book. Maybe the title grabbed your attention, maybe a friend told you about it, maybe something inside you said, "I need this right now." Whatever the reason - Thank you.

Thank you for being here with me.

There are vivid memories from my childhood, most of them not so good, many of them terrifying. There are parts of me I used to compare with my daughter, thinking, *if only she knew what my childhood was like, she wouldn't be acting this way.* That's what I believed before I woke up to awareness. Now, I see it differently.

That's why I'm telling you my story. Because when you finally realize that things are not what you've been told, not what you've always believed, you start breaking those patterns, and everything shifts.

And maybe you think your story is bad. Maybe you think, *you have no idea what I've been through*. But wait. Because once you start the journey of awareness, once you hear the stories of others, you'll see something powerful: you're stronger than you realize. Your brokenness and your past do not define you.

The moment you start consistently working on your mindset, daily, something inside you changes. Your perception shifts and that change becomes unstoppable.

That's what this book is about.

It's about survival.

Opening my wounds, not to bleed, but to show you what healing looks like. It's about finding the courage to love myself, truly, for the very first time.

So, let's begin.

"THEY SAY TIME HEALS ALL WOUNDS. IT DOESN'T. TIME JUST TEACHES YOU HOW TO CARRY THE SCARS AND THE PAIN WITHOUT SHOWING THEM ALL THE TIME."

Lina Langford

The Door

I remember standing in front of that big brown door. Mahogany. Heavy with gold hinges.

We waited...Just stood there...Waiting for someone to hear us knock.

When I close my eyes and think about that moment, it feels like we stood there forever. Like time stopped. The door had nothing fancy. Just a small peephole where we peeked from the inside, trying to guess who was knocking.
A few scratches from years of hands that came and went.

A gold doorknob that could break if you pushed too fast. The neighbor's door was fancier, more modern.
But my grandparent's door...It had a heartbeat. I could feel the air and I can still remember the smell of the walls. Plain white walls that looked like they needed a fresh coat of paint.

That wasn't just a door. That day was a turning point. It was the moment my life tilted upside down.

Because when that door opened, I was about to lose something I didn't even know I could lose - my identity.

My sense of safety. My idea of love, care, and protection.

And from that day on, everything I thought I could trust, everything I thought would protect me was gone.

No matter how hard I worked, how much I tried or how much I wanted it, from that moment on the direction of my life would be in the hands of one person. One person who decided what was "best" for me. That person was my mother.

And the truth?

I was at her mercy. Completely. My entire life depended on her.

And nobody, nobody was coming to save me!

My brother was standing on my right. My mother was on my left. She kept pressing the doorbell repeatedly. We were on the second floor and every ring felt like another reminder that something had ended and something new, something harder was about to begin.

Finally, my aunt opened the door. She looked surprised. Really surprised. She just stared for a moment before calling out to my grandmother, "Mother!"

And then my grandparents came toward us. My grandmother appeared first, right there by the door. My grandfather stood back near the kitchen. My grandma smiled, but it wasn't a full smile. It was hesitant, like she knew right away that we hadn't shown up to say hello. We were there because something was wrong.

That three-bedroom, one and a half bath house felt huge to me. The family room was all the way at the back of the hallway. My grandparents' bedroom was off to the left. And near the front door, there was this big living room with beautiful furniture, but it was for guests only. Not for daily use.

We didn't sit in the big room. We all gathered in that small family room in the back. My grandpa had the old coal heater going, and it was warm. Comfortable. But inside? None of us were comfortable.

I didn't know what to say. My brother was silent. I was even quieter. And then my mother... She erupted.

"He left us for that bitch!" she screamed. No tears. Just anger.

She wasn't sad, she was furious. Furious that he had walked out. Furious that the woman he left for wasn't even "beautiful enough". To her, it was an insult. I was only six years old. My brother was three. We were the ones who would pay the price because he left. She was going to use this against us for the rest of our lives.

I didn't fully understand what was happening, but I knew this: my mother was broken, my brother was lost, and I... I was sad.

That day, in that room, with that coal heater humming and my mother's voice echoing, we weren't just visitors in my grandparents' house.

We were a family starting over, whether we were ready for it or not.

Grandma's Kitchen

Grandma's house was warm in a way my mother wasn't. It wrapped around you like a soft blanket on a cold day. She wasn't an overly affectionate lady, she didn't smother us with hugs or kisses, but she had this quiet, steady, and soft kindness. You could feel it in the way she moved, the way she made sure we were fed, the way she looked at us with her beautiful hazel eyes like we mattered. My grandfather was the same. He didn't say much, but when he did, there was a gentleness that felt rare in our world. But he was also quick to get mad.

The heart of the house was the kitchen. Always. The kitchen sink was on the right side, right by the balcony door. From there, you could see my grandparent's garden and the two neighbors in the next building. The fridge was on the left, tucked behind the door.

There was a small table on the left too, not always used for eating but more for preparing meals, chopping vegetables, and getting dishes ready for the family.

The smell of home cooked food drifted through the air, bread toasting on the old coal stove each morning, spices filling the hallway, something always simmering on the stove. That smell carried a message:

You are safe here. You will not go hungry.

Still, there was always a shadow in the background. Grandpa's eyesight was fading. His cataracts clouded his vision, making the world around him blur. Yet, he was the only breadwinner in the house.

Money was tight. We didn't live comfortably, not in the way some families did. But here's the thing, we never lacked food. Not once.

Fish from the local market. Fresh vegetables. Warm bread from the bakery. I still remember the smell of it. Simple meals, but every bite was made with care. Nobody, absolutely nobody could cook like my grandmother.

Grandpa used to say, "She puts love in everything she makes."

And I believed him. Because you could taste it.

We lived by the sea, so seafood was always cheaper and it made everyone in the family happy.
Fresh fish, green salad, and rice became the most common meal in that kitchen, simple and perfect; that's the way my grandmother cooked. Every meal began the same way. We would gather for dinner, grandpa always started meals with blessings and gratitude to God, and he left the table with gratitude, too.
It was his quiet reminder for us that everything placed in front of us was a gift.

Grandma always started with soup. Then came the main dish. My grandma cooked okra sometimes. I hated okra. Even though hers was barely slimy, I almost gagged every time I ate it. Then rice. Ended with dessert most nights. She'd set the salt on the side, even though we rarely needed it, her food was already perfect.

We didn't have much, but when we ate, we ate like we had so much.

I never once thought of us as poor when we were eating. How could we be? The food wasn't just food. It was comfort. It was love. It was proof that even in the middle of hardship, beauty could exist.

Looking back now, I see it so clearly. The kitchen was more than a place where meals were cooked.

It was the heart of survival.

Grandma's food taught me something I didn't realize until much later: even when life takes away safety, love, and certainty, you can still create warmth. You can still find rituals that keep you grounded.

We didn't have money, but we had meals that tasted like love. We didn't have stability, but we had moments that felt like home.

And that's the paradox of trauma: you can live in chaos yet still find small pockets of comfort that carry you through. For me, it was toasted bread on the coal stove and its irresistible smell, soup simmering on the stove, and the quiet kindness of a grandmother who gave without words.

It's why, to this day, food will always mean more to me than just nourishment.

It represents survival.

Connection.

A reminder that love doesn't always shout, it often whispers, right from the kitchen.

Grandpa's Eyes

Grandpa didn't see well. His world was a blur, a place where shapes move like shadows and colors bled into each other. But he never complained. He never showed frustration or sorrow. Instead, he relied on me.

I was his eyes.

When we went shopping, I became his guide. I described everything to him: the colors of the fruit, the bright red tomatoes, the green plums, the beautiful bright apricots with freckles on their skin.

Cantaloupe was his favorite. Back then, you could smell the fruit before you even reached to grab it. He could tell just by the smell. I told him about the people walking past us, though to him they were nothing more than shadows, even me. But he knew my voice. He even knew the way I breathed.

"Step up. Step down. There's a rock, move to the left. Turn right. The watermelon today is very red, Grandpa. The sky looks dark, it may rain, we should hurry today."

I didn't think about it much; it's just what I did. What I've always done. Holding his hand as we navigate the streets felt natural, like breathing. It was not a burden, not a chore. It was love.

I never held my mother's hand the way I hold Grandpa's. Not because I didn't love her, but because the way I held his hand was different. There was a purpose to it, a silent connection that words could never explain.

His hand was warm, strong, yet fragile in a way that made me hold on just a little tighter. He trusted me completely, and in that trust I felt something deep inside me, something that made me proud, made me want to protect him the way he has always protected us.

But Grandpa was not just wise, he was funny. A man with a spirit too big for his aging body.

His favorite trick? His dentures.

Whenever he wanted to tease us, or when he wanted our full attention, he simply popped them out. Just like that. No warning. One second he was talking, and the next his teeth were in his hand with a big smile.

My brother and I reacted the same way every time; laughter, shock, discomfort, all rolled into one. We laughed because it was funny, we felt uneasy because it was strange, and we got a little mad because, somehow, he always caught us off guard.

And Grandpa? He just grinned. His toothless smile was full of mischief, knowing he had won.

Even with his blurred vision, even with all his struggles, he found a way to make us laugh. And maybe that was the most important thing of all.

Because life wasn't always easy. But if we could still laugh, we knew we would be okay.

A Full House, A Heavy Heart

The plates keep coming. One by one, they are added to the big aluminum tray in front of us. The room is filled with voices, the clinking of spoons against bowls, the quiet hum of life moving forward, even when things feel uncertain.

Our family isn't small, at least, not right now. My mother sits across from me, tired but silent, her mind elsewhere. My brother sits beside me, eating quietly. My aunt is here, too, but tonight she is not alone. She has a man with her and we all already know who he is. But his presence changed the air in the room this time.

She's about to tell the whole family how much they're in love. The problem is, he's also a cousin. His presence means more than just another plate at the table. He was going to stay with us for a little while.

I could read the worry and sadness on my grandmother's face the rest of the night. Her sister's son and her daughter were in love and she couldn't stop it. A love so deep, so certain, that no amount of disapproval from my grandparents could shake it. They wanted to be together, no matter what. And no matter how hard my grandmother and grandfather tried to reason with them, to warn them, to convince them otherwise, they stood firm.

"I love him," my aunt said.

"And I love her," he replied.

And that was that.

The house is full, yet there is an emptiness in the air that lingers like an unspoken truth. Days are passing, but not in the carefree way they used to. The laughter is quieter, the conversations more hushed.

My mother finally finalized her divorce. Each day, she moves a little closer to cutting ties with the life she once had. She carries the weight of it in her shoulders, in the crease between her brows, in the way she stirs her tea without drinking it. She doesn't talk about it much, but I can feel it. We all can.

And then, one afternoon, everything erupts.

I don't even know what is happening until I hear the yelling.

My father is at the door.

I stand frozen in the hallway; my breath caught somewhere between confusion and fear. His voice is loud. My mother's is louder.

I didn't understand the words at first. I only understand the anger.

It fills the space like fire, spreading through the house, consuming every corner. My mother is furious. Not just upset, furious in a way I have never seen before. Her voice shakes the walls.

She is tired.

She is done.

She doesn't care who hears, who sees, or even how we feel.

I want to say something. I want to make it stop. But I am just a child standing in the middle of a storm I don't understand.

My brother grips my hand, his fingers small but tight around mine.

No one notices us. No one asks if we are okay.

Because in this moment, nothing else matters except the fight at the door.

And for the first time I realize: love is not always warm. Sometimes, love burns. Sometimes, love turns into something unrecognizable.

And sometimes, love is not enough to keep a family whole.

I don't remember every word that was said, but I remember the chaos, the way my grandfather kicked him out, yelling for him never to come back. My mother's voice filled the air, screaming at everyone, at my aunt, at my grandmother. My brother and I cried until our throats hurt. And my father...for a moment, he was there for us. But the house was too loud and too full of anger for him. He wasn't wanted there and he did not want to fight for us. That was the last time he ever stepped foot inside.

And then he was gone. For good.

As the days passed, my mother grew angrier. More bitter. My brother was just a little boy, active, playful, too young to understand the rules of silence. But in my grandfather's house, silence wasn't just expected, it was demanded. Especially during the news at 7 and 8 p.m. You didn't dare interrupt. Not a whisper, not a sound.

My brother couldn't sit still. And that's when everything turned dark.

I remember my mother grabbing him, dragging his tiny body down the hallway. His feet scraping against the floor. His little voice, panicked, screaming. *"No, Mommy! No, Mommy! Hurt, Mommy!"*

She pulled him into the guest living room, the one we weren't allowed to use, the one with the perfect furniture reserved for outsiders. And then she locked the door.

She locked it so no one could get in.

Not me.

Not Grandma.

Not anyone.

I pounded on that door, crying, begging her to stop. I yelled, *"Take me instead, Mommy! He's little. He's just a boy mommy!"*

But she didn't show mercy. Not that night. Not ever.

I didn't need to witness every hit to know what was happening behind those doors. I recognized the rhythm. She probably grabbed his arm or his hair with her left hand, pulling him close enough so he couldn't move and hit wherever she could land.

When she finally stormed out, his little body was limp with exhaustion. He was too tired even to cry anymore. His tears stained his face and his voice was gone. I remember holding him, rocking him, whispering, "It's okay, I'm here."

But it wasn't okay. It was never okay.

That was the night I begged God for the first time. Not for myself, but for my brother. My grandmother used to say that if I opened my hands to the sky while praying, God would see me and hear me more. So I would open my hands wide, stretching my fingers as far as they would go just to be sure He could see me. I prayed harder than I ever had. *Please, God. Please save him. Don't let this be his life. Take me instead. But save him.*

I was only a child, but in that moment, I learned what it felt like to carry someone else's pain.

When I look back now, I see two children trapped in a cycle that was never ours to begin with. My brother's cries, my desperate begging, my prayers whispered in the dark, they all came from the same place: a child trying to protect another child when no adult would.

That memory stays with me, not just because of the fear, but because it was the moment I realized what love really meant. Love isn't just pretty words. It's not promises. It's sacrifice. It's saying, *"Take me, not him."*

But the tragedy is this: love was what we gave each other as children. Protection was what we tried to give each other. And the adults, the ones who should've protected us, didn't.

That kind of betrayal changes you. It hardens parts of you, but it also plants something powerful- the will to survive.

And that's what my brother and I did. We survived.

I don't remember when my mother started beating me the way I remember her beating my brother. His first violent punishment is burned into my memory forever.

But mine?

I can't recall the first time. Maybe my memory wants to erase it. Maybe it's my brain's way of protecting me. What I do remember is that the beatings were constant. Daily. Brutal. Our tiny bodies could not handle it.

And my mother...she looked as if she had no emotions at all. No anger. No regret. No softness. She was like a robot, moving through the motions of violence as if it was her duty.

My grandfather thought the answer was marriage. He wanted her to get married again. Maybe then she would be happy. Maybe then it would relieve her of the rage that consumed her and in turn, relieve us. But no matter what he said, she refused. She had bigger dreams or at least that's what she told herself. Dreams that didn't seem to include us, at least not in the way we wished they would.

I lived in fear. My head always throbbed, pounding even on the days she didn't raise her hand against me. I carried the fear everywhere.

Sometimes it was the smallest things. My grandfather kept a garden. Fruit trees, fig trees specifically. If I took one too soon, before it ripened, I paid for it with bruises. I was punished for wanting sweetness too early.

When it became too much, I would run to the pasture across from my grandparents' house. I'd sit in the grass, alone, and talk to God. I was only a child, but I spoke to Him like He was my only friend.

I told Him my dreams.

I would take a stick and draw in the dirt, my house with a roof and two children: a boy and a girl. My children. And I would whisper a promise: *I will never hurt them, God. Never. Please, just give me a loving home.*

That was my prayer. That was my dream. Not money. Not things. Just love. Just peace. Just a house where no one was afraid.

I think about that little girl often, the one drawing houses in the dirt, praying to God for children she didn't even have yet. That little girl was broken, beaten, humiliated and terrified. And yet, she was already choosing differently.

I didn't know it then, but every prayer I whispered in that pasture was me rewriting my story. Every promise I made to God was a seed planted for the life I live now.

It's strange how pain can teach you love. How being beaten can teach you compassion. How being neglected can teach you the importance of being present.

And while my mother's dreams didn't include us, mine always included the children I didn't even have yet. Because even in the middle of the storm, my heart knew what I wanted: a safe home filled with love.

There's a pain that sits so deep in your chest, it feels like it was stitched into you before you even knew how to speak.

That's what my childhood gave me. Not memories you can point to like photographs, but scars that live in the silence between heartbeats.

I grew up learning that love could hurt, that trust could vanish overnight, and that safety wasn't something you could count on. I learned that sometimes the people who are supposed to protect you are the very ones who break you. And when you're a child, you don't have a choice, you carry it, you swallow it, you survive it. If you are lucky, you will make it!

It took me decades to understand it myself:

What breaks you is not what defines you.

I was beaten. I was silenced. I was betrayed. For years, I thought that was the sum of who I was, broken pieces of someone else's hatred. But I see it differently now. Those things didn't define me. What defined me was what I did with the pain.

I loved my brother when no one else showed him mercy. I prayed to God for a different life when no one else gave me hope. I dreamed of a loving home even when I had never lived in one.

That's who I am. Not the bruises. Not the tears. Not the fear.

And maybe that's what survival really is, not just making it through the storm but holding on to a vision of a life that doesn't exist yet, and refusing to let it go.

I won't lie to you. Healing is not pretty. It doesn't tie up nicely with a bow. Some wounds never close all the way. Sometimes I still feel like that little girl crying outside the locked door. Sometimes I still hear my brother's voice begging. Sometimes I still feel the sting of betrayal when I remember my father walking away.

But here's the miracle: even with a heavy heart, I rise.

Even with scars, I choose love. Even with broken beginnings, I am building something whole.

So, if you're carrying pain, if your story feels too heavy, let me tell you this: You are not what happened to you. You are what you choose to create after it.

And if a little girl with bruises on her body could sit in the grass and draw a dream house in the dirt, promising God she'd one day give her children a safe home, then maybe you can take the heaviest pieces of your story and turn them into something beautiful.

The Neighbor's Son

We had neighbors. Some closer than others. One of them beat her children, too, almost like it was a competition with my mother. Who could strike harder, who could hurt more. Violence was so normal in our world, it lived in the walls of those two buildings.

On the first floor, there was a family with two boys. Their mother was pregnant, an "accident" with twins, one boy and one girl. We were close, the kind of neighbors who walked into each other's homes without knocking or slipped in when the door was cracked open. It was normal. Normal enough to blur the lines of safety.

The oldest son started touching me. His hands wandered where they didn't belong and rubbed me in places that made my skin crawl. My body froze each time but my mind screamed.

Every time I tried to pull away, he whispered the same threat. *"If you tell anyone, I will tell your mother."*

And that was enough. That was worse than the touching. The thought of my mother finding out and her beating me for something I hadn't even done choked me. My throat closed every time he said it. I could feel it, like I was suffocating.

So, I didn't speak. I didn't fight. I just let it happen.

He would pat the burgundy velvet sofa, telling me to lie down next to him. My stomach turned as I obeyed, too terrified to say no or move.

When I look back now, I whisper, *Thank God it was only touching.* But at the time, there was no gratitude. Only fear. Only shame. Only silence.

What do you do when the place you live in doesn't just allow violence, but normalizes it? What do you do when the people who should protect you become your prison?

I was a child who learned early that silence was my shield. That speaking the truth would only bring me more pain. And that's the cruelty of growing up in abuse, you stop trusting your own voice. You swallow it. You bury it.

That boy didn't just steal moments of safety from me; he reinforced the lie that I was powerless. He taught me to believe my body wasn't mine, my boundaries didn't matter, and my silence was the only thing keeping me alive.

But here's the truth I see now: silence may have protected me then, but my voice is what saves me now.

I tell this story not because it's easy, but because every time I speak it out loud, I take back a piece of what was stolen. I refuse to let the weight of someone else's shame choke me anymore.

To anyone who has lived through something like this, let me say this clearly: what happened to you is not your fault. Your silence was survival, not consent. Your fear was real and it was valid. But you are more powerful than the people who tried to control you.

That little girl lying on the burgundy velvet sofa thought she had no choice. But the woman I am today knows that I do. I always have a choice. To heal. To rise. To speak.

And I will never again let fear lock me into silence.

My grandparents begged my mother not to beat us like that. They begged often. Their broken voices shook with desperation, but nothing ever reached her. Their words were soft, fragile like whispers thrown against a storm.

And my mother... she always had the same response.

Cold. Final.

"They are my children. I am their mother. I can do whatever I want. They are mine."

Mine. Like we were objects. Not children. Not human. Like bags of vegetables she could toss around, bruise, or throw out when she was done.

That's what we were to her, something she owned. Not someone she loved.

I remember one day so vividly, it has never left me. My mother said we could go outside and play, as we always did. The weather was warm and the streets felt safe, the kind of safety you only believe in when you're a child. It was close to dinnertime but I wasn't worried. I knew my rhythms. I knew when to eat. I wasn't late. I wasn't doing anything wrong.

I was only one block down, playing with friends, laughter bouncing around us like music. Then I heard it.

Her voice.

She was calling me from the back of the house with that tone. That sharp, cutting tone. The one that froze your blood before the first blow ever landed.

I knew. I knew instantly. I knew the purpose of her voice. I knew what was waiting for me.

I ran. My feet hit the ground hard, my lungs burning, trying to get back to the house before the punishment. But she was already there. Already in the street waiting for me. Already ready for war.

She grabbed me by my hair. My long hair, my pride as a little girl, twisted violently around her wrist. She dragged me across the street, her voice was so loud it cut through the entire neighborhood.

I screamed. I begged. But there was no mercy.

The pain was blinding. Every root felt like it was exploding out of my scalp. My head was on fire, my skull throbbing so hard I swore blood was going to pour out of me.

She dragged me straight into the house. My grandmother rushed to the door, begging, her gentle hands trying to stop her, her voice shaking. But my mother shoved her aside.

I can still hear my grandmother's powerless sobs as the door slammed and locked behind me.

The guest living room again.

Always that room.

The room with the furniture that wasn't even meant for us. That was where punishment lived.

She pounded on my back, fist after fist, my hair still wound around her wrist like a weapon. She slammed my head into the wooden armrest of the chair. I hated those chairs. I hated the way the wood felt against my skull, my forehead, the way it seemed to watch me like it knew it was part of my pain.

My face. My head. My arms. My back. Every inch of my body screamed. The pounding pain swallowed me whole. I couldn't breathe, couldn't think, couldn't fight.

I can still physically feel it in my lungs when she beat me, the way my organs shook inside me, the way my head used to pound. I still remember.

And then, as suddenly as it began, she stormed out. My body was a heap, too broken to move. My grandmother was waiting at the door, her voice breaking as she begged.

"You will kill them one day...you know."

But my mother's face was blank. No emotion. No remorse. Hurting us wasn't even about anger anymore, it was her purpose. And my only mistake? I didn't hear her the first couple of times she called my name.

Her favorite words weren't *I love you* or *Goodnight*. They were, *God damn you. May God curse you. May God send you to the deepest place in hell.*

That was the kind of lullaby I grew up with, the curse my mother sang to me all those years until it sank into my bones.

That memory doesn't fade.

It lives in my body, even now. Every time my scalp aches, every time my back stiffens, I remember the way her hand wrapped around my hair, the way pain felt like fire burning through my veins.

And here's the truth that hurts the most: it wasn't just the pain. It was knowing that my grandmother's begging couldn't save me. That no adult could. That no one would.

There is a particular kind of loneliness in being beaten in front of people who love you but are powerless to stop it. It teaches you that the world can see your suffering and still leave you alone in it. That's a wound deeper than the bruises.

But as I sit with this memory now, I don't just see the girl who was dragged by her hair. I see the girl who survived it. The girl who screamed but never stopped fighting inside. The girl who, even with a pounding head and a broken body, still clung to hope that one day she would not live this way anymore.

It breaks my heart to think about her, because I know she didn't deserve it. None of us did. And if you've lived through something like this, if you've been dragged, beaten, or silenced, you didn't deserve it either.

The scars I carry remind me of what I went through, but the fact that I can write these words today, with my heart heavy but still beating, reminds me of what I overcame.

I was not killed.

I was not broken forever.

And even though she tried to make pain my purpose, I found my own.

And my purpose is this: to live, to love, to choose myself, and to break the cycle so my children will never know what it feels like to be dragged across the street by their own mother's hands.

The Gift of Gratitude

As I grew older, my bond with my grandfather began to change. We connected in a way that felt different from the rest of the world. As I mentioned before, he couldn't see well, his cataracts clouded his vision, but I became his eyes. I was his guide, his little helper. He leaned on me more than anyone, and in return, he gave me something I didn't even realize the value of at the time: Trust.

He didn't have much to offer. Money was tight, life was heavy, and he carried the weight of being the only provider in a house full of needs. And yet, he always tried to make me happy with the little things he did have.

And that mattered.

I felt it, even as a child, the quiet gratitude between us. It was a bond made not of grand gestures or big words, but of small, steady acts of love.

Both my grandmother and grandfather taught me something that has never left me. Something that carried me through nights of bruises, through mornings of fear, through days when hope seemed far away. Something that money could not buy.

They taught me **gratitude.**

Not the shallow kind of gratitude people throw around casually when they say, "be thankful," "look on the bright side." No. What they showed me was deeper. They taught me that even if you don't have much, you can still give. And that when you give with a sincere heart without expecting anything in return, the good will always find its way back to you.

Every night before bed, they reminded me: *Pray. Give thanks. Always thank God before you close your eyes.*

So I did. I prayed. I whispered gratitude.

I didn't always understand it.

How could I give thanks when my head was pounding from my mother's hand? How could I say *thank you* when my scalp burned from being dragged across the street, when my arms and back were sore from her blows, when my heart ached from silence?

Sometimes I wondered if I was doing it wrong. Was gratitude just words you said out loud? Or was it something deeper, something I was too young and too broken to grasp?

I prayed anyway. Every single night. I prayed with tears still drying on my face. I prayed with bruises still fresh on my skin. I prayed because they told me gratitude was the way through.

And even if I didn't fully understand it then, something about those whispered prayers carried me.

Now, looking back, I see the truth of what my grand-parents gave me.

They gave me survival; not through money, not through protection, but through perspective. They planted a seed in me that I wouldn't see grow until I became older: the power of gratitude.

Gratitude isn't about pretending life is perfect. It isn't about denying the pain or covering the bruises with nice words. Gratitude is about finding the hint of light in the darkest night and holding onto it like your life depends on it because sometimes, it does.

I understand now what I couldn't then: gratitude is not easy. It is not natural when you're hurting. But it is powerful.

When you can whisper "thank you" with a heavy heart, you're teaching yourself to see beyond the suffering. When you can still give with nothing left in your hands, you're proving to yourself that you're not defined by what was taken from you.

My grandparents couldn't stop my mother's rage. They couldn't erase the violence or heal the wounds. But this lesson of gratitude was the tool that helped me survive it.

Gratitude is not about ignoring the pain. It's about refusing to let the pain blind you to the moments of love that still exist.

And that's why I can say today, with tears in my eyes and truth in my heart, that I am deeply grateful for them.

Grateful that they showed me a path, however fragile.
Grateful that they taught me to pray when I didn't know what else to do.

Grateful that they gave me a way to keep going when everything in me wanted to stop.

The power of gratitude is something many people never figure out. But I did.

And I owe it to them.

"THE HARDEST AND MOST CHALLENGING PRISON TO ESCAPE IS THE ONE BUILT BY YOUR OWN FAMILY, WHICH YOU NEVER CHOSE IN THE FIRST PLACE."

Lina Langford

The Unchosen Child

There were times when my grandfather tried to give me up for adoption. That was the only way he knew how to save me. He saw what was happening. He saw what my mother was doing. His hands were tied in so many ways, but this was his rescue attempt.

And God knows how much I wanted that.

Imagine being a child so desperate to be free, you long for strangers to take you in. I didn't dream of toys, or dresses, or anything children normally hope for. My dream was freedom. My dream was safety. My dream was to be anyone else's daughter, anyone's if it meant I didn't have to belong to her anymore.

But my mother wouldn't allow it.

Not because she loved me. Not because she couldn't bear to let me go. But because of pride. Pride was her anchor. To the outside world, she wore a mask of a woman who could play her role, smile when expected, charm the neighbors. Inside the house, it was different. Inside the house, her hands only knew how to land blows.

There was one woman who wanted me. An old lady who had never had children of her own. She was sick and near the end of her life. And all she wanted, all she asked for was to spend her remaining years with a girl she could call her daughter. She wanted to leave her belongings, her legacy, her love to someone.

She wanted to adopt me.

I wanted her too. I wanted her so badly it hurt. It didn't matter that she was old. It didn't matter that she was sick. I would have gone with her in a heartbeat, without question, without fear. Because even a dying woman's home felt safer than living under my mother's roof.

Unfortunately, that chance slipped away. She died soon after. Just like that, the little flicker of hope vanished. Even if she had lived, I probably would have ended up back in my mother's hands anyway. That was the pattern. No matter how close freedom came, it never stayed.

It's a strange thing to admit but survival sometimes means wishing for an entirely different life even if it means leaving behind everyone you know. I didn't want wealth. I didn't want comfort. I wanted peace. I wanted to wake up without fear.

As a child, I couldn't name it but now I can. I wanted to be chosen.

Not tolerated. Not kept because of pride, not beaten into silence, not insulted repeatedly. I wanted someone to look at me and say, *"You are mine, and I want you, I love you. I won't hurt you!"*

That's the wound that never fully heals, the wound of not being chosen by the person who should have loved me first. And yet, it's also the wound that gave me strength. Because when you grow up unchosen, survival becomes your choice.

I chose to keep going.

I chose to find meaning in the smallest scraps of kindness.

I chose to believe that someday, somehow, I would belong somewhere safe.

I wasn't adopted by that old woman, but I was adopted by life itself. By resilience. By strength. By a God who heard me even when I thought He was silent.

Sometimes salvation doesn't come the way you hope. Sometimes it comes in whispers. In endurance. In the refusal to give up.

That's how I survived the unchosen life. By choosing myself even when no one else did.

A Love That Wasn't Ours

There was a time when my mother almost got married.

Or at least, that's what we all thought.

I remember him standing inside our front door. He leaned down toward me, his blue eyes fixed on mine, and he said softly, *"From now on, you can call me Daddy."*

That moment has never left me.

Because for a child who never felt safe, who never felt chosen, those words meant more than he probably ever understood. For one flicker of a second, I wanted to believe him. I wanted to believe that maybe, just maybe, this was the man who would finally protect me. The one who would see me. The one who would save me.

But deep down, I think I already knew. Nothing in my world was ever that simple.

He was handsome. I can see him in my memory even now, his hair combed neatly back, his orange-brown mustache, his confident presence. My mother fell for him quickly. Maybe she needed someone to lean on. Maybe she thought he would give her the life she believed she deserved.

But as always, her choices weren't about us. Her desires, her hopes, her plans, they were only ever for herself.

She would leave us behind to spend nights with him. Weekends, too. My grandfather hated it. He despised the way she disappeared, leaving her children under his roof, under his rules, while she pretended to live as if she didn't have responsibilities.

Neighbors tried to justify it. They told my grandfather that this was normal, that young women needed to enjoy life. Some even covered for her, pretending she was with them instead of gone with him. But the truth couldn't be hidden forever.

One day, she found out he was already married. He had two children of his own and a wife who had no intention of leaving. He was a man who introduced himself to other women as single, long before my mother came along.

It all unraveled.

And while my mother may have been shattered by the discovery, I didn't care. My pain was already louder than hers. My bruises, my fear, my silence. They mattered more to me than her heartbreak over another lie.

She thought she almost had love. But it was never ours to share.

Children don't just watch their parent's choices, they carry them.

When he leaned down and told me to call him *Daddy*, it wasn't just words. It was a seed of confusion planted in a heart already breaking. I waited for someone to claim me, to love me, to step in and say, *"You're safe now."* But instead, I got another reminder that stability wasn't mine to have.

My mother's life was hers to chase. Her pride, her loneliness, her hunger for love, her ego, it consumed her. And her children were never in the center of it. We were always in the shadows, watching. Waiting. Wishing.

That's the hardest part of growing up in a house like mine: realizing you are never the priority. That your safety, your happiness, your very childhood can be put on hold for someone else's need to be wanted.

Your worth is not measured by the love someone failed to give you. Your story does not end with their rejection, or their betrayal, or their abandonment, or their selfishness.

I was never anyone's first choice. Not my father's, not my mother's, not this man at the door. But I chose myself. And that choice has carried me further than any broken promise ever could.

So, if you've ever been overlooked, overshadowed, or left behind: You are still worthy. You are still enough. And no one's absence can erase or change the truth.

The Hair She Loved, The Pain I Hated

My hair was never just hair.

To my mother, it was her grip. Her weapon. Her way of dragging me, controlling me, humiliating me. She loved to wrap my long, shiny hair around her wrist as if it were jewelry, as if it gave her power. And in a way it did.

To the outside world, my hair was beautiful. Long, shiny, and flowed down my back. People complimented it. My mother herself used to say, *"I love your hair, it is very beautiful."* She said it with pride, as though my hair was her accomplishment.

But to me? My hair was a curse.

Every night when I tried to sleep, my scalp throbbed. The roots pounded as if they carried the memory of every time she had yanked them, every time she had dragged me across a room, every time she had wrapped her hand in them to remind me that I was hers to hurt. My head was on fire, even in silence.

My hair wasn't a crown. It was a chain.

She had a ritual, wrapping my long, beautiful hair around her wrist as if it were some twisted comfort, a sick kind of relaxation for her.

One of my friends once said something to me, *"If you cut your hair short, she won't be able to wrap it around her wrist anymore."*

That idea burned in my mind like a tiny flame of hope.

So, I begged. I begged my mother every single day to cut my hair. I thought maybe, just maybe, if it was gone, she couldn't hurt me that way anymore.

But she refused. Every time.

"But I love your hair. It is very beautiful," she would say.

She loved it because it was hers to use. I hated it because it was mine to suffer.

I begged until my voice grew tired and when my words weren't enough, I turned to my grandmother. I recruited her to help me. I needed someone else to see my desperation, to plead with me.

Finally, together, we wore my mother down.

And she cut it.

My long, shiny hair fell to the ground, and for the first time, I felt like a piece of the weapon she had used against me was gone.

But even then, it wasn't freedom. Because she never let me forget it.

For the rest of my life, I would hear it. *"She had beautiful hair, shiny and long. And all she did was beg me to cut it."*

Those words carried blame, as though I had ruined something precious. As though I had been ungrateful. As though I had destroyed beauty instead of trying to save myself.

Let me tell you something about survival. Sometimes it doesn't look noble. Sometimes it doesn't look like strength. Sometimes it looks like begging for your hair to be cut off just so it can't be used against you anymore.

And yet, that is strength. That is survival. That is what it means to fight with the scraps you're given.

I didn't want short hair because of a style. I didn't want short hair because of rebellion. I wanted short hair because it was the only way I could dull the pain. The only way I could sleep at night. The only way I could reclaim one tiny part of my body from her control.

It's strange, isn't it? How something as simple as hair could hold so much meaning. For her, it was power. For me, it was pain. But in the end, it became a choice.

Cutting my hair was not just about scissors and strands on the floor. It was about me saying, *I will not carry this weapon on my head anymore. I will not make it easy for you to hurt me.*

And even though she tried to turn it into a story about loss, I know the truth.

Cutting my hair was the first small victory of my life.

Because sometimes survival is not about winning the war. It's about winning one battle.

One night of sleep without pain. One piece of yourself reclaimed.

That haircut was mine.

My choice.

My freedom.

And even though she never understood it, I did.

IF YOU WANT CHANGE, STOP BLAMING YOUR PAST. THE PAST IS OVER AND UGLY, BUT EXCUSES ARE UGLIER AND THEY LIVE IN THE PRESENT."

Lina Langford

A Reason to Be Loved

With the man at the door, the one she wanted to marry, my mother tasted freedom. And she wanted more.

We lived in the suburbs. She talked about finding a job in the city, about moving there, about starting her own life. My grandparents didn't oppose. They knew the years were passing, that she couldn't stay under their roof forever. Maybe they thought this would be the turning point, the chance for her to become independent, to settle, to provide for us.

But my sweet grandmother was worried. She was especially worried for me. We were growing up and my cursed hair was slowly getting longer. By then, my mother stopped beating my brother. Her focus had shifted and her anger had found a new home: Me!

I wasn't her daughter. I wasn't her child. I was her competition. I was the girl who mirrored her face, her femininity, her presence. And in her eyes, that made me her enemy. I wouldn't fully understand this until years later. But I knew, even then, that she saved her worst for me.

She found a job at a local insurance agency as a secretary. The man who owned it was tall and remarkable. He was the kind of man people noticed; powerful, sharply dressed, polished shoes, hair always in place. You could spot him from blocks away because he looked different, better, more refined than the others. My mother fell into his orbit very quickly.

Time passed and suddenly there was talk of a beauty salon. My mother introduced it as his business, something she would help manage. But as I grew older, I would remember the paperwork, the signatures, the licenses. It was never his. It was hers. She wasn't just managing it; she was the owner. No one really knew the truth. The shop was only a rental, but opening a beauty salon is not easy, especially when you had nothing.

And everyone was happy for her. Finally, she was building something. Finally, she had a place in the world beyond the shadows of my grandparents' house.

By then, I was in middle school. Old enough to know what was happening, too young to escape it. The beatings hadn't stopped. If anything, they wore me down more than ever. I was exhausted and angry, not just in my body, but in my spirit.

My grandmother and grandfather eventually moved to the city, too. They wanted to be closer to us. Close enough that when I banged on the wall for help, or when I begged the neighbors to call her, my grandmother could rush over and pull me out of the fire. She tried, over and over, to rescue me when no one else would.

But even with her, I wasn't myself anymore. The girl I was meant to be had been beaten out of me.

I remember one day, standing in the living room. The window was cracked open and the curtain moved softly with the wind. I don't know why that detail stays with me, but it does. Maybe because the curtain looked free in a way I never felt.

My mother was there. Something inside me rose up that day, some scrap of courage I can't explain.

"Mom...don't you ever love me? Even just a little bit? Because if you did, you wouldn't beat me like this."

She looked at me without any emotions. Her body still, her face unreadable. And then her voice cut through the air like a blade.

"Tell me one thing I should love you for. One single reason. Give me a reason to love you."

I can still hear it. The sharpness. The coldness. The way her eyes looked at me, empty of warmth, empty of anything but disdain.

That was the moment I knew for sure that I wasn't loved by her, not even a little.

And something inside me broke.

Because if your own mother can't love you, who can? If the person who brought you into this world looks you in the eye and demands a reason to love you, what does that make you? Unworthy. Unlovable. Nothing.

That's the thought that sank its teeth into me that day. And it followed me for years, whispering into my heart no matter what I achieved, no matter how good I was, no matter how hard I tried. *Why would anyone love you?*

My grandmother always ran to me and she did that day as well. I can still hear her on the stairs, how fast she would climb, rushing because she heard my screams, my begging to my mother. A neighbor must have called her again. They always did. She would come, angry and shaking, and she would say, "One day you're going to kill this child. She will die in your hands, your own daughter."

And then she would take me to her house. I'd sit on the floor, rest my head on her knees, and she would run her fingers gently through my hair. With her small, chubby, gentle hands, she comforted me. I never wanted her fingers to touch the roots of my hair, because they hurt so much, the pain was still raw and she knew it. She was careful. She wouldn't touch my scalp; instead, she gently patted my hair and gave me a comfort I'll never forget.

My hair wasn't even as long as it used to be but she still hit my head and neck hard, grabbing whatever she could and it always hurt so bad.

"Grandma, why is my mother like this?" I would ask her.

"I don't know, my girl," she would say. "Your mother is different...She breaks many hearts and the price of that will weigh heavily on her. I don't know why she turned out this way."

She was a mother, too. And she didn't know where to place herself, or where to place her child.

Maybe you've asked yourself the same question. Maybe someone in your life made you believe you weren't worth loving. And if you've ever felt that weight, you know how it crushes you from the inside out.

When a parent rejects you, it feels final. It feels like a verdict written into your skin. You carry it everywhere, like an invisible brand. And it doesn't just hurt in the moment—it echoes, it repeats, it shows up in every relationship, every decision, every doubt.

I spent years trying to prove my worth. Years trying to be good enough, kind enough, strong enough, beautiful enough, anything that could answer her question. Anything that could finally give her a reason to love me. This became my identity.

You will never be able to earn the love of someone who has closed their heart to you. And their inability to love you is not proof that you are unlovable. It is proof that they are incapable.

It took me decades to understand that. To separate my worth from her rejection. To realize that love isn't something you beg for, it's something you're worthy of simply because you exist.

That day in the living room, when she told me to give her a reason, I didn't have an answer. I stood there with nothing. But if I could go back, if I could speak to that little girl again, I would take her hand and whisper:

"You don't need to give anyone a reason to love you. You already are the reason. You are enough. You are worthy. And one day, you will know it."

The Ghost Who Reached for Her Father

My grades were falling. I couldn't focus on anything in school. I was physically there, sitting in a classroom, walking down hallways, but my mind was gone. I was drifting through life like a ghost, invisible even to myself.

I was about 13 years old, still just a kid. But I was old enough to feel the emptiness of wanting more, old enough to see a small glimpse of hope out there somewhere. Or maybe it wasn't hope at all. Maybe it was just a wish. A wish that somehow, somewhere, someone would notice me. Someone would care. Someone would save me.

I started talking back, raising my voice at her but never enough to stop her. Just enough to make her even angrier. I gave up on school. I just stopped trying. How could I learn multiplication tables when my head throbbed from the night before? How could I write essays when my stomach twisted from hunger?

I didn't have money to eat lunch at school. I didn't have good food to bring from home. My mother never packed a lunch for us. I don't remember her ever walking me to the school gate, kissing me goodbye, or hugging me when I came home. That's not the mother I had. I walked to school alone and I walked home the same way.

We used to visit another city sometimes, where my grandfather's older brothers lived with their families along with my great-grandmother. On one of those visits I couldn't hold it in anymore. I opened my heart to my grandfather's younger brother's wife. I told her everything. How badly my mother was beating me. How tired I was of the pain. How much I wanted my father.

She looked at me with kind eyes and listened. She told me she didn't know exactly where my father was living, but she knew where his uncle lived. Just two blocks away.

The moment she said it, tears spilled out of me. I panicked. I wasn't ready for it. I didn't expect it at all. I begged her not to tell him, not to do anything. Because if my mother ever found out, she would beat me until I couldn't stand. I was terrified. My fear was bigger than my hope.

But this woman, she promised me. She comforted me. She said it would be our secret.

She arranged a visit, quietly. I sat across from my father's uncle and his family. They were kind. They cared. They looked at me not as a burden, I was just a child in need. They told me they felt sorry for me, that no child should go through this. They promised they would reach out to my father, that they would tell him where I was, that they would ask him to come and find me.

And for the first time in so long, I let myself imagine it, my father coming back. My father walking through the door. My father saving me. It was a desperate kind of hope but it was all I had to hold on to.

I waited. Every day, I waited. That was my secret time, my private hope that one day soon he would show up and everything would change.

One afternoon, I was coming home from school. Like I often did, I stopped by the beauty salon before going home. I always wanted to see if my mother was there before I walked into the house, because I knew her moods better than anyone. Most of the time, she was at the insurance office, so the salon felt safer to check first.

I climbed the steps to the second floor, toward the office. And that's when I saw her.

My mother.

She was standing still at the door, waiting. Her face was hard, her body stiff. And I could see the madness burning inside her like fire, like steam pushing out of her nose and ears. I froze. I knew instantly. She had found out.

She knew I had reached out to my father.

Not because the family betrayed me. Not because I told anyone else. But because my father had called the office. He said he wanted to see us.

That single phone call ruined me.

God knows how much I was punished for that. The beating, the rage, the endless screaming. My body carried the bruises, but my heart carried the real wound. Because from that day forward, I wasn't just punished, I was blamed.

It became another weapon in her hand, another scar in my memory. She reminded me of it repeatedly. That I had dared to want my father. That I had dared to hope for rescue.

And in her eyes, that was my crime.

Sometimes the worst punishment isn't the beating. It's the way hope itself is used against you.

I wanted my father. I wanted someone to see me, to save me. That's not weakness. That's what every child deserves. But in my world, even that small, fragile hope became another reason to suffer.

That's what trauma does. It teaches you that reaching out will cost you more than staying silent. It convinces you that even the things that should save you- your father, your voice, your truth, will only bring more pain.

For years, I carried the guilt of that day. I believed it was my fault. If I hadn't said anything, if I hadn't cried to that woman, if I hadn't wanted too much, maybe my life would have been easier.

But here's the truth I see now: it wasn't my fault.

It was never my fault.

A child should not have to beg for safety. A child should not have to beg for love. A child should not be punished for wanting a parent. A child should not carry shame for speaking the truth.

I know that now. But back then, I didn't. Back then, I learned a different lesson: that survival sometimes means shrinking your hope so small that no one can find it, not even you.

And maybe that's why I walked like a ghost because carrying hope felt more dangerous than carrying pain.

But I'll tell you this, because I believe it with everything in me: hope always finds its way back. Even if it's buried, even if it's silenced, even if it's punished. Hope doesn't die. It waits.

And though my father never came for me, and my mother punished me for wanting him, the hope I carried then is the same hope that carried me into the woman I am now.

That ghost became flesh again.

That silence became a voice.

That hope became survival.

The Words That Bruised Me

It wasn't only the beatings.

The bruises on my skin eventually faded. The pounding in my head dulled after a while. But the words? The words never left. They lived inside me, echoing long after she stopped speaking.

My mother's tongue was just as brutal as her hands. She used it like a weapon, cutting me down repeatedly. She told me I looked like a bitch. She told me I was going to be a prostitute or worse, that I already acted like one.

Do you know what it does to a child to hear that from her own mother? To be called dirty, worthless, shameful before you even understand what those words mean? It sinks into your bones. It settles on your soul.

She never missed a chance to complain about me to everyone around us. To relatives. To neighbors. To anyone who would listen. She wanted the world to know how unlucky she was to have me.

She would say how other people's daughters were smarter, prettier, better. Every other girl was something to admire and I was the mistake.

"Everyone else got good daughters. Look at mine. Look at what I'm stuck with."

That was her poem. The role she played over and over, so loud that even when she wasn't speaking, I could still hear it inside my head.

And I believed it.

When your mother tells you you're worthless, you believe her. When she tells you you'll never amount to anything, you believe her.

When she compares you to everyone else and tells you that you are the disappointment, you believe her.

That's the cruelest part of verbal abuse. You don't have to see the bruises to carry the scars.

Maybe you've heard those kinds of words, too. Maybe not the exact same ones, but words that told you that you weren't enough. That you were unlovable. That you would never measure up.

Verbal abuse isn't always visible. No one sees it when you walk down the street. But it's there, living in your chest, poisoning the way you see yourself. The wounds are invisible, but the damage is real.

I was just a kid, but all I could think about was finding my soulmate. That was my escape plan. I should've been in school, focused, learning, dreaming. But I wasn't. I thought the only way out was through love. If I could just find someone to love me, to be mine, then I'd finally be safe.

Now I know better. But back then, I didn't know that.

What I did know is I was starving. Starving for love, starving for kindness. I wasn't mature enough to see the better way out. Education, success; those were the real doors. But I was too young, too blind, and too desperate to notice.

I remember every time we visited neighbors or anyone we knew, I would beg her the entire way there. *Please, Mommy, don't complain about me. Please don't tell them what I did wrong. Please, Mommy, I feel so bad.* I begged, but it never stopped her.

For years, I carried my mother's words like they were the truth. I wore them like a uniform. If she said I was nothing, then I was nothing. If she said I was shameful, then I was shameful. I didn't question it. I let her voice become my own.

But those words weren't mine to carry.

They belonged to her. To her anger. To her emptiness. To her brokenness. She spit them at me because she couldn't handle her own pain, her own failures, her own disappointment in herself. I see that now.

But back then, those words built walls around me. They silenced me. They convinced me that no matter what I did, how hard I worked, how much I tried it would never be enough.

And yet, here I am.

I am not the names she called me.

I am not the shame she tried to bury me in.

I am not the disappointment she put on display in front of the world.

I am proof that words can wound, but they do not have to define you.

If you've ever been called less than you are, if you've ever been made to feel small by the very person who was supposed to lift you up, I want you to hear this: *You are not their words. You are not their judgment. You are not their shame.*

You are yours. And you are enough.

"I THOUGHT MY BROKEN PIECES AND MY MISTAKES MADE ME USELESS. TURNS OUT, THEY MADE ME STRONGER THAN I EVER IMAGINED."

Lina Langford

The Last Time I Saw My Father

A few months later my father came to visit us.

His presence filled the room in a way that stopped me in my tracks. He was tall, handsome and older than I remembered. He wore brown, neatly ironed pants, pressed so perfectly they had sharp creases running down the legs. I still remember the way the fabric looked under the light, smooth and crisp. Black sharp looking shoes.

He let me sit on his lap. I climbed onto his left leg and folded my hands together nervously, rubbing them as though that motion could calm me. He asked me how I was doing.

But I couldn't answer.

I didn't dare raise my head. I couldn't look into his eyes. I couldn't look at my mother either. Because I knew the moment I did, the moment I met his gaze, I would collapse. I would burst into tears, wrap my arms around him, and beg him to take me away.

I couldn't risk it. Not with my mother sitting just a few feet away, at her desk, calm, silent, and waiting for her time. Watching me. Watching us.

He knew I couldn't say much. He knew words were dangerous for me in that room. So, he suggested lunch. He wanted to take us out, just for a little while.

My brother didn't want to come. He didn't remember my father the way I did. He was angry and resentful. He had become the "good child" in my mother's eyes, the one no longer beaten, the one fed with her stories. He was the golden child. She told him our father was an evil man who had abandoned us, and he believed her. He stayed behind.

But my father looked at me, and I could feel he wanted time with me. He wanted to talk.

We walked to the coffee shop together.

What we didn't know was that my brother had followed us. He came in silently, sat down next to us without a word. My father didn't push him away. He only smiled softly and held my hands, lifting them to his lips and kissing them gently.

He told me how much he had missed us. His voice was kind. Understanding. Patient. Maybe he made it look like he cared. He tried to explain my brother's distance. *"He is a boy, you know. He tries to protect his mother,"* he said.

And then I couldn't hold it in anymore. I told him I wanted to go with him.

The words hung in the air. Heavy. Desperate. Final.

He went quiet. He stayed quiet for a long time, searching for the right words. I held my breath. My whole future was balanced on his response.

Finally, he said he didn't know if it was possible.

He told me he had a family. A wife. Two children. He would need to talk to her. He wasn't sure.

My shoulders collapsed under the weight of his words. I can still feel it now, the way my body slumped, the way my chest tightened, the way my spirit sank. Another person didn't want me. Another person couldn't choose me.

And the voice inside me whispered the same question I had been carrying for years. *Why would anyone love me? Why would anyone care for me?*

He took us shopping that day. Bought us a few things. I smiled for him. I was happy for those little moments. But underneath, I was shattered. Because I knew the truth: he wasn't going to take me with him.

We went back to the office.

That night, when we went home my mother's boss also came to our house for dinner. My mother said it was important that he needed to be with us, so if my father showed up he would protect us.

My father had left.

Dinner came and went, and I thought that was it.

But then—bang, bang, bang—someone knocked at the door, loud and urgent.

I looked through the tiny hole. My breath caught in my throat. "My father," I said out loud.

Everyone froze. Everyone stood up.

My mother began screaming, shouting accusations into the air. My father's voice roared back. "I need my daughter!"

And my mother screamed: "You can't have her!"

I was shoved back, pushed away, hidden. But I knew the end of this story already. I knew I would pay dearly for this night.

Someone called the police.

I ran to the balcony. I needed to see him. I needed to see with my own eyes what was happening.

My mother tried to pull me back inside from the balcony.

"Stop crying for him," she snapped at me. "Cry for me."

I was gripping the cold metal bars, holding on tight. She tugged at me again, trying to drag me back in, and I shoved my shoulders forward fast, just to make her let go. That's when she hissed, "Go to hell."

The street below filled with flashing red and blue lights. Neighbors poured out of their homes, whispering, pointing, watching. Two officers held my father, one by his arm, the other by his head. They led him away like a criminal.

And then, just before he disappeared, he turned. He looked back over his left shoulder. His eyes searched for me or maybe that's just what I wanted to believe.

And I saw it. His sadness. His defeat. His love, tangled with helplessness.

That was the last time I saw him.

He was gone for good.

This was not just a goodbye. This was the shattering of a child's last fragile hope.

When your father comes back and tells you he misses you, holds your hands, kisses them and then admits he cannot take you it breaks something inside you. When you watch him walk away in the hands of police, dragged like a criminal, while your mother screams like the victim it destroys the part of you that still believed in rescue.

That night, I learned something I wish no child would ever learn, sometimes the people who love you cannot save you. They can be your worst enemy.

That truth haunted me. It whispered into every empty space in my life. *You are not worth fighting for. You are not worth staying for. You are not worth choosing.*

And here's the thing about survival: even when the world tells you you're worthless, somehow you still find a way to keep going. Even when love walks away, you cling to the tiniest fragments of it, enough to carry you through one more day.

I didn't see my father again. But I remember his eyes that night. The way he looked back for me even as he was taken away.

That look became my anchor. Because even if he couldn't save me, even if he didn't take me, for a brief moment, I saw it: I was loved by him for a split second.

And sometimes, that tiny glimpse of love is all a child needs to keep surviving.

My father was not innocent by any means. I'm not trying to say he was a great father, but I have no real opinion of him other than the fact that he left us. I have other memories with him, too. Ones I choose to keep to myself for now.

Yes, he made a mistake leaving us for another woman. He could've fought for us, could've protected us, even against my mother's anger.

But he didn't.

And my mother. She kept us, she fed us, she dressed us, she kept a roof over our heads. But she destroyed us at the same time. She destroyed us so severely that we carried the price on our backs every single day.

He made one mistake.

My mother however, never stopped making them.

And I still don't know which one is worse.

The Game of Pain

A fter my father was gone for good, something inside me broke.

That last glimpse of him, the sadness in his eyes as the police led him away, was the final thread of hope snapping inside my chest. If he couldn't save me, no one could.

As a result, I built a new belief for myself: the only way out, the only way I could ever be safe, was if I found the right person to marry. If I could find someone – anyone - who would take me, love me, and keep me safe, maybe I could escape.

I started searching for him in my mind at such a young age, far earlier than any child should. I didn't care if he brushed his teeth. I didn't care if he had a job. I didn't care if he wasn't even 18 yet. None of that mattered. The only thing I dreamed of was becoming a family, of being wanted, and of being loved kindly.

Every night, before I fell asleep, I closed my eyes and did what my grandparents taught me. I prayed. I showed gratitude. I whispered "thank you" for blessings I hadn't even received yet. And then I dreamed. I dreamed of a wonderful husband and two children I would love and care for with every ounce of my being. I dreamed of happiness that felt impossible in real life, but alive in my imagination.

But while I was dreaming, things at home were shifting again.

My mother's boss began visiting more often, especially on Friday nights. He was around so much that it became almost normal, his presence added another layer in the story I didn't know how to make sense of. They were fighting so much. Every Friday night ended with screaming. Some nights he stayed, some nights he stormed out. And after my father was gone, my mother turned her rage back to me physically, verbally, relentlessly.

But this time, something inside me snapped in a different way.

The first time she came at me again, I did something I had never done before: I raised my hand. I held her arm in mid-air.

I was trembling. My chest was pounding so hard I could barely breathe. But I held her arm.

And for one second, I felt something unfamiliar, pride. Power. The tiniest spark of strength.

But right alongside it came terror. She looked at me differently this time. Not just with anger, but with shock. Then, she completely unraveled.

She began to hurt herself.

I watched as she dug her nails into her own skin, starting from under her chin and dragging them down toward her chest, leaving red streaks on her neck and chest. She pounded her fists against her chest, slapped her own face repeatedly.

She screamed at herself. *"I'm a bitch. I am. I know I am, I am a slut."* Then she beat herself harder.

I stood frozen at the door. My heart split in two. Part of me didn't know what to feel. Should I feel relieved that, for once, she wasn't hitting me? Should I feel good that the pain was hers this time? Or should I feel terrified of what I was witnessing?

But none of those emotions came. Instead, I felt something worse. I felt sorrow.

I began to cry. I begged her to stop. *"No, Mommy, you're a good mom. Please don't hurt yourself."*

But the more I begged, the harder she went. She clawed at herself, beat her chest, screamed louder. And I didn't know yet, but this was her new game.

This was the next chapter of her cruelty. She would beat me first. Then, when she was done with me, she would turn her rage on herself, knowing I would beg her to stop. She knew that I cared, that I loved her even as she destroyed me, and she used that against me.

She enjoyed it. She fed on my begging.

And some days, after she fought with her boss, she turned on herself. She didn't touch me, but she beat herself instead. And I would beg her to stop.

Then she would run toward the window, pretending she was going to jump. We were on the fifth floor. I was terrified. She never jumped, but every time she acted like she would, and every time I begged her not to. That became her new way.

She even did it in front of her boss. She would hit herself so hard her chest turned bright red, almost purple. Spit flew out of her mouth as she screamed and clawed at herself. I was scared of how she looked, like she wasn't even human anymore, but I still begged her, over and over, to stop.

And I learned something dangerous in those moments. I learned that hurting yourself could bring attention. That pain could make people care. That if I ever wanted someone to notice me, maybe I needed to harm myself, too.

That was the trick she taught me without ever saying a word.

This is the twisted legacy of abuse: it teaches you not only how to suffer, but how to repeat the cycle inside yourself.

When I raised my hand to stop her, I thought I had found strength. And for a moment, I did. But she twisted even that into another way to control me. She turned pain into a performance, into a game where my love for her became my weakness.

And here's the part that hurts to admit. I believed her. I believed her words about herself. I believed her words about me. I believed pain was proof of love and that maybe if I hurt myself too, someone might finally see me.

That's how deep it goes. That's how abuse rewires a child's mind.

But looking back now, I see something else, too. Yes, I learned her trick. Yes, I could feel how easily it could pull me in. But I also see the strength it took for me to beg her to stop. Even when she beat me, even when she screamed at herself, even when she told me I was unlovable, I still begged her to stop hurting. Because my heart was still alive. My love was still alive.

And that, I realize now, was my saving grace.

Abuse can twist you, but it cannot erase your humanity. It cannot kill the part of you that still loves, that still hopes, that still dreams.

I didn't want to learn that pain equals love. But I did learn something else: I could survive anything.

And survival, even in the darkest places, is its own kind of victory.

The Day Shame Became My Skin

I was so young. Too young to know what was happening to my body. I had just started my period and no one explained anything to me. There were no pads back then like girls have now. My mother just told me, "Find some old fabric, cut it, and use that." That was it. No comfort. No guidance. No kindness.

Sometimes, I was beaten just for that.

For cutting the wrong cloth.

For not knowing what to do.

For bleeding, something I didn't even understand yet.

She never taught me what it meant to become a woman. She never told me this was normal, that I wasn't dirty, that I wasn't wrong. All I got was yelling, insults, and shame.

I remember after a bath or going to the bathroom, I would hide the used cloth behind the bath stove, thinking, *I'll grab it later.* But I was a child, I forgot sometimes. And every time I forgot, she exploded. She screamed at me, called me disgusting, cursed me.

One day, it was towards the evening. I will never forget this. She was already furious with me over another cloth. She was screaming, and then the door opened and her boss walked in. He came by often, but this time, he walked right into her anger.

He asked, "Why are you yelling like that again? What happened?"

She grabbed his arm. "Come. I will show you."

My heart stopped. *No. She won't. She wouldn't do that to me. Not in front of him. Not this.*

But she did.

She dragged him toward the bathroom, ignoring his resistance. He didn't want to go. But she pulled him anyway. And then, in front of the bathroom, she pointed and shouted.

"She leaves her dirty, bloody rags behind the bathroom door. She stinks up the place!"

I wanted the ground to swallow me whole. My face burned. My ears rang so loud.

Even now, writing this, I can feel the heat rushing back into my cheeks, the shame crawling up my neck. I was already embarrassed and lost in something I couldn't understand, and she made it a show.

How does a mother do that?

How does a mother humiliate her daughter like that?

I don't even know how many times things like this happened. Too many to count.

Too heavy to carry. People talk about one traumatic moment that shapes them forever. Some have only one. I had hundreds. Sometimes I still wonder if I dreamed it, if maybe it was all some nightmare. But then I feel it again, the fire in my face, the humiliation flooding me and I know it was real.

That was the night shame became my skin.

And it has never left me.

Hungry for Love

The years were slipping by, and with every season that passed, I grew lonelier. The kind of loneliness that sits in your bones, the kind that makes you feel invisible even when you're surrounded by people. My mother had a new friend then, and soon weekends meant visiting her house.

That house carried a darkness of its own.

One night, I woke up under my blanket to a weight that didn't belong there and hands that weren't mine. Her friend's son had slipped in. His hands touched me where I didn't want to be touched. I flinched, I tried to move, but he pressed me down with a force stronger than mine.

His breath was hot against my ear when he whispered, *"If you make any noise, I'll tell everyone you invited me under the blanket."*

I froze. I didn't scream. I didn't fight.

Because I knew what would happen if I did. My mother would never believe me. She never did. She would blame me. Punish me. Hurt me worse than he ever could.

So, I let him touch me.

We had so many grownups around us, my mother, her friend, her husband. Still, no one noticed. He wasn't invisible, but it was like nobody saw him. Even now I wonder how. Being a mom myself, that would be the first thing I would notice.

I don't know how many nights it happened. I lost count, maybe on purpose. But I remember when it ended, when my mother fought with her friend and the visits stopped.

That was my escape, not anything I did.

I remember whispering, *"God loves me,"* as though He had pulled me out of fire. But the burns were already there, inside me.

The Kiss Before Death

I remember the first time I fell in love. I was 14. He had the most beautiful hazel eyes. His smile—God, his smile lit something in me I didn't know existed. Straight white teeth, a warmth that made me wonder why I had never noticed him before. My mother had owned that salon for a while, but somehow this was the first time I *saw* him.

My heart felt like it was going to explode. Maybe he was the one who would save me. Maybe he was God's gift to me. I don't know how many excuses I made just to walk past his shop, just to catch his eyes, just to see that smile. Every time he looked at me, it felt like the world stopped.

If you looked out the window or from the balcony of my mother's beauty salon, you could see part of him, his legs, his hands and sometimes I could even catch him leaning forward, looking over to see if I was there.

I started wearing more makeup after I noticed him, trying to impress him. Burgundy lipstick, red lipstick. I wanted him to see me. My mother caught me one day, lipstick still fresh on my lips. She looked at me and sneered. "You look like a whore."

I was so used to those words by then.

"No, I'm not," I would say back. "I'm not a whore."

She'd play her word games, twisting it. "I didn't say you *are* one. I said you *look* like one."

But it didn't matter. He never looked at me like that. Not once.

One day he told me he had someone in his life. He had been dating her for two years.

"Two years?" I asked. "That's a long time. I wish someone loved me for two years."

He smiled, almost apologetic. "You're too young. But you're so beautiful. If I didn't have her, I would be yours."

My heart sank. I was crushed. I hid away for a couple of weeks, heartbroken. But I couldn't stay away. I still passed his shop, still hoping for that smile.

And then one day he told me they had broken up. I thought, *See? God loves me. God is on my side.* Now he was closer, and so was I.

He told me he was leaving for a summer job in a beach town. He said, "Wait for me." And of course I would. I would wait forever.

The day before he left, he held my hand and kissed me, not quite on my lips, not just on my cheek - right in between. My heart dropped into my stomach. My entire body shook.

I ran to my grandmother's house. "Grandma, something happened," I said, panicked. She looked at my face and saw my fear.

"What is it, baby?" she asked.

"I think I'm pregnant," I whispered.

Her hazel eyes were wide open. "What? When? What happened?"

I pointed. "He kissed me right here. When do you think the baby will come?"

For the first and only time, I saw every emotion on my grandmother's face at once - fear, anger, relief, sadness. She exhaled, sat me down and explained that wasn't how it worked. But at that moment, I had truly believed it.

The next morning, I walked to the shop, but something was different. People were standing outside, faces heavy. They looked at me with sadness. My stomach sank.

"What happened?" I asked.

No one spoke. Finally, an older man told me. "You didn't hear? He died last night."

My body froze. "What? No...No...What happened?" I was crying, sobbing and couldn't hold it.

"A truck with no headlights hit his motorcycle. Killed him instantly."

Less than five minutes after he kissed me...he was gone.

I collapsed, sobbing. The only person who ever made me feel love - gone. My first love. My only hope.

Later, after his burial, I learned he had been wearing two bracelets. One with his name. One with mine. My heart broke all over again, but at the same time, it made me feel something I can't explain, like maybe he had loved me in his own way.

I tried to end it after that. I swallowed a bunch of pills.

I didn't die.

Instead, my tongue swelled so badly I couldn't speak.

And my mother? She didn't hold me.

She didn't comfort me.

She wasn't even scared for me. She said I embarrassed her. She was just angry. Angry because I ruined her weekend plans. She shoved me onto a bus, told me the doctor said I'd be fine.

"This is what you get for your stupidity," she said.

HOW I SURVIVED UNBROKEN

Everyone else had loving mothers.
And that was mine.

"I'M NOT LIVING IN THE PAST LIKE THEY SAY. I'M JUST NOT BLIND ANYMORE. I SEE HOW UGLY THEIR HEARTS ARE AND HOW PRESENT THEIR GAMES STILL ARE. I KNOW THE TRUTH, AND I WON'T PLAY ALONG ANYMORE."

Lina Langford

Buying My Place in the World

I lied a lot when I was younger. I spun false stories about myself of grand families, important ancestors and royalty in our bloodline. I told people my great-great-grandfather had been someone important.

Why did I do it?

Now I know it was because I needed to feel like I was somebody. I needed to believe I came from something bigger than the small, broken corner of the world I was trapped in. I needed attention. I needed love. And if I couldn't get it by being myself, I would invent someone worth noticing.

Because deep down, I never felt worth it.

My mother never packed our lunches. Never kissed us goodbye at the door. Never sent us to school with a smile or stick a note in our pocket. Other kids had those things. I didn't. She was too busy chasing admiration from others. Outside, she looked like one person. Inside, to us, she was someone completely different.

There's only one memory of her showing up at my school. It was high school. My teacher had called her in because I had started acting out and spending money I usually didn't have.

It's embarrassing to admit now, but I was stealing.

By then, my mother had a new fiancé, a rich engineer, handsome, never married. He felt sorry for her, or maybe he loved her. But he stuffed her wallet with cash like patching holes in a leaking roof. She had more money than ever but she never gave it to us. Not freely. Not with love.

So, I took it.

I learned to slip bills from her wallet when she wasn't looking. Small amounts, just enough so she wouldn't notice. Enough so I could feel like I had control over something, anything.

And for the first time in my life, I felt power.

At school, I bought myself toast and a Coke for lunch. Simple. Ordinary. But to me, it was everything. Food that I chose. Food that was mine. Food I didn't have to beg for or starve without.

But I didn't stop there.

I bought lunch for my friends, too. I shared what I stole. And suddenly, I wasn't the hungry girl anymore. I wasn't invisible. I was generous. I was important.

And just like that I became popular.

Overnight, people noticed me. They laughed with me, they called my name, they wanted to sit with me. My friends loved me or at least it felt that way.

And I soaked it in, desperate. Because for once in my life, I wasn't the disappointment. I wasn't the ghost hiding in the corner.

For once, I was someone.

And all it took was money.

The Day I Ran

I don't even remember what I did that day. Maybe nothing. Maybe I breathed wrong, looked wrong, spoke wrong. Maybe she didn't want me to go out with my friend. She called all of my friends whores, too. It never really mattered.

She called me a bitch. She always did. Those words were her favorite weapon. They cut sharper than her hands.

But once again, I found myself being beaten.

As I always did, I clutched the back of my neck tightly, right where my head met my spine. That became her favorite spot after she cut my hair. She struck me there over and over, like it was her target, the bullseye of her anger. My hands tried to shield it, but they never really could.

She screamed names at me. Ugly, filthy words I can't even write down without feeling the sting all over again.

Her voice was poison, her fists relentless.

And then something twisted happened. She grew more furious because her hands began to hurt. Every strike against my body left her palms aching, and instead of stopping, she punished me harder for that. As if my skin, my bones, my body were guilty of the pain in her hands.

What a mess.

A nightmare that made no sense, except in her world.

When she was finally done with me, she turned on herself.

She dug her nails into her skin, clawed at her chest, pounded her fists against her body. She screamed the vilest names at herself, names I don't even want to repeat even now, decades later. Watching her was like watching someone split in two, someone completely consumed by darkness.

One day, after finishing with me, my brother walked into the room.

She turned to him with her wild eyes and said, *"Son, deal with her. Beat her so bad that she wouldn't be able to backtalk me ever again."*

I froze. My body was already broken, but those words shattered something deeper.

In that moment, he could have chosen me. He could have said, *"No, Mommy, she's my sister. I love her."* He could have stepped in, been the shield I needed.

But he didn't.

He looked at her, then at me. *"Mother, if I beat her, she would lose her life in my hands."*

I am now almost fifty years old and I still remember those words. Word for word. They will never leave me.

I left the house. My body bruised, my spirit gasping. I was running, not walking, not sneaking, but running for my life. My legs carried me down the street, desperate, shaking until I found myself near the coffee shop.

My friends were there. A small group of boys and girls I often hung out with. We weren't bad kids, just teenagers trying to pass time, trying to laugh, trying to feel alive.

I walked up to them, tried to act normal, tried to smile through the storm raging inside me. I opened my mouth to speak, to explain, but before I could even finish a sentence, my friends pointed.

My brother was coming.

He walked toward us with purpose, his face hard, his steps heavy.

And then he hit me.

Right there. In the street. In front of everyone. Blow after blow as if I wasn't his sister, as if I wasn't even human. My friends stood by, silent. They tried to step in, they could only call his name, telling him to stop.

The humiliation burned hotter than the pain.

I cried as he struck me, cried as the world blurred with shame and betrayal. No one stopped him.

No one.

Eventually, I stumbled home, my body aching, my spirit completely undone. I cried harder than I had ever cried before. Sobs tore out of me so violently that no one in the house could quiet me. I cried until there was nothing left in me but exhaustion and resolve.

I packed a small handbag, slipped money out of my mother's things because survival required stealing and I walked out the door.

Not for a moment. Not for a night.

For good.

I was done.

The City

Here I was, not even seventeen, walking the streets of a big city I didn't know. My tiny handbag, the only thing I carried, grew heavier with each step. The streets buzzed with noise and strangers rushing past me, but all I felt was exhaustion. Not fear, though I should have been afraid. Just hunger, weariness, and the hollow ache of needing a place to belong.

I wanted to go home. But not *that* home. Not the place I couldn't even call home anymore.

I wandered until I found a small music store. Through the window I saw a chair, empty, like it was waiting for me. I pushed the door open, stepped inside, and asked the girl behind the counter if I could sit down.

She smiled gently and said, "Of course." Then she looked at me, really looked, and asked, "Are you hungry?"

I whispered, "Yes."

Her next question cracked me open. "Are you okay?"

I broke. My body shook with sobs I couldn't hold back. Tears streamed uncontrollably, unstoppable, pouring out years of silence.

She leaned closer and said softly, *"Tell me. I want to help you."*

And so I did what I had done before: I told a story. Not the truth, at least, not the full truth. My story came spilling out as if it had written itself inside me. I told her I had just come from Germany. That I was married. That my husband was supposed to join me a week later. That my bag had been stolen at the airport with my money and ID inside. That I had nothing left.

None of it was true. But I said it with the conviction of someone who needed it to be believed.

Earlier that day, I had stopped at a little jewelry store and bought myself a cheap wedding ring, slipping it on my finger so strangers might see me as married, as protected, as off-limits. I thought maybe it would scare someone away. But I'm sure I still looked sixteen. A child pretending to be grown.

The girl's eyes softened with sadness. She believed me. She took me to her home.

And here's where I still believe in angels. Not the kind with wings. The kind that walk quietly among us, opening doors when we need them most.

The Angels

Her family was poor. They lived in a tiny, worn down one-story house that looked like it had seen better days. The kind you might pass by without noticing. But inside, there was warmth.

Her mother cooked simple meals, and there was kindness in the way she placed food in front of me. The father was tough but not cruel, serious, yet steady. The girl had two brothers, but to my relief, they never tried to touch me. Not once.

No one shouted at me. No one beat me. For the first time in my life, I slept in peace.

I began to believe I had truly been delivered to angels.

But angels can't always shield you from the world.

One morning, I woke up, stretched, and blinked against the morning light. And then I froze.

She was there.

My mother.

Sitting at the side of the bed. Her new fiancé beside her.

I shut my eyes again, hard, as if I could erase her by pretending it was a nightmare. But when I opened them, she was still there.

The family had gone to the police, quietly. They had heard my mother's report of a runaway girl and realized who I was. They had meant well, trying to return me to where I "belonged."

But I didn't want her there.

In my heart, I screamed. *Why did you come? Why couldn't you let me go?*

I sat up and faced her. My voice shook as I asked, "Why did you come?"

She narrowed her eyes and said, "What do you mean, why? I came to take you home."

I cried, "I don't want to go anymore. I'm so tired. You beat me all the time. I don't want to be hurt anymore."

For once, she promised. "I won't beat you."

I whispered, "And my brother?"

She said, "Your brother, too."

And just like that, I was going back home.

A New Cycle

A t first, things softened. She didn't beat me as much. She got married, and life shifted into a new rhythm. But the cost was my childhood. My dreams. My sense of safety.

Yes, there were good days here and there. But most of them existed only for show, for neighbors, for friends, for strangers who believed her act. She needed to look good in public. She needed to shine, to be admired. I was often the mirror she used to reflect her beauty.

When I was in my twenties, we walked together down the street. People would stop and compliment her. *"You don't look like a mother at all. You look so young, so beautiful."* And every time, she turned to me and asked them, *"Well, which one of us looks like the mother? Which one of us looks like the daughter?"*

Do you know what humiliation feels like when it comes wrapped in a smile?

That was it.

I am skipping so many traumas here. I could fill pages with them. But I am not here to tell you every single beating, every single silence, every single wound. I am here to tell you how I survived. To tell you that you can survive, too. That cycles can break.

When she married him, eventually I began to call him Daddy. He was kind, gentler than she ever was. He had generosity in him. But he was also her greatest enabler.

When we were together, I used to beg my mother. "Please, Mom, please don't tell him we fought again. We fight over such small things, things that don't even matter. Why do you make them such big deals? Why do you complain about me to him? Please, Mom, just one day—don't tell him we fought."

But no. The moment he walked through the door, she started poisoning him. She told him things I never did, words I never even said. She was always doing just enough to make me look crazy, while she stayed calm, played the victim. I never understood why she always did that or why he always believed her.

She never showed him her real face, not for years. Maybe every now and then a piece of it slipped through, but not enough. Now he finally sees it, but it's too late.

To this day he is powerless. He is her biggest enabler. And he's lost himself so much in her world that even his own identity is gone.

All these years, she kept insulting him under one excuse or another. He was fat, unintelligent, bald, she said he needed a hair transplant, but it was too late, that his belly was too big, and so on. Then she would ask their friends to tell him and encourage him to lose weight, pretending it was for his health.

But the truth was, she simply didn't think he was good enough for her, she even told me that several times. Yet she always hid behind the same excuse.

"It's for your own good, my love."

No matter how kind he was, he still believed her lies. He still took her side. He never beat me like she did, but once he kicked me, once he raised his hand. And always, he supported her.

If he hadn't, she would have made his life hell. So, he chose the easier path standing with her, against me.

Her power grew with him. And though the bruises faded, the humiliation, the insults, the silence, the abandonment those cut just as deep, if not more.

Every now and then, someone would suggest she owed me an apology. She would smirk and say, "Am I supposed to apologize to the shit I pushed out of my own ass?"

I didn't hear this once by accident. I heard it multiple times, over and over.

Let that sink in.

I Wish I'd Given Birth to a Stone

Some mothers sing lullabies over their babies. Mine sang curses.

I wish I'd given birth to a stone instead of you. May every drop of milk I ever gave be poison to you. May it rise up in you and make you suffer for the rest of your life.

I hope you rot in the deepest pit of hell.

That became my lullaby, the words I heard over and over through the years. A sentence sharp enough to cut skin, spoken by the one person who was supposed to protect me. She didn't mutter it in anger and regret it and apologize later. She said it like she meant it, as if I were truly a mistake, a burden, something less than human, many times.

I still remember her face, the spit flying from her mouth as she threw those nasty curses at me.

At some point, I stopped seeing her beauty. People used to call her attractive, they still do. They admired her hair, her figure, the role she played very well, her smile. But to me, none of that mattered anymore. Beauty dies when you've seen the darkness in a person's heart.

All I saw in her was cruelty.

Childhood was one set of scars. Youth was another. By the time I hit my twenties, she couldn't hit me as she once did. Her hands weren't as strong anymore. But her cruelty didn't stop. She simply found new weapons. The slaps turned into humiliation. The bruises turned into abandonment. The rage turned into silence that lasted for days.

She performed her pain in front of me like a theater. She'd dig her nails into her own chest, leave bloody marks, and scream that I was killing her. She'd open the car door mid-argument while I was driving, as if she might throw herself out while I begged her to stay.

She fed on my begging. She wanted me to beg, wanted me to feel guilty for her threats, wanted me to believe I was the cause of her suffering.

And it worked.

I had two father figures in my life. My biological father, who walked away. My stepfather, who chose to stand beside her instead of protecting me.

Two fathers and I was left alone with both.

But God, He gave me something else later in life. He gave me a husband. A man who loves me without conditions. A father to my wonderful children who is gentle and steady.

A partner who reflects back to me what love actually looks like. And once you see real love, once you feel gentleness, you cannot unsee it.

I cannot pretend cruelty is normal anymore.

Still My Mother

When I was in my twenties, I finally went to college. I was older than the rest of the kids there because I started later. But I was proud. I made it. I thought maybe I could finally build something for myself.

One day, she came to visit me. And as always, we fought. That was our rhythm, always circling, always clashing. Even if we laughed, even if we shared one tiny moment of peace, I knew it was only temporary. I always knew the price would come after. Laughter never lasted in my world.

We left my apartment together, walking down the street. On the corner was a beauty salon where everyone knew me. I don't even remember what she was mad about. With her, the reasons never mattered. She turned to me and said sharply, "If you act like this, I'll just go back."

I was tired. I looked at her and said, "I didn't do anything wrong. If you want to go back home, then go."

That was enough. That was more than enough.

In a flash, she spun around and slapped me across the face so hard I hit the wall. My face stung, but worse than the sting was the shame. The men from the shop saw it. They came outside and said, "Lady, what are you doing?"

I wanted to vanish. I wanted to disappear right there on that street. My chest was tight, my throat closing.

The humiliation burned hotter than the slap.

I ran back to my apartment, shaking. I told her to leave, to go back home. But she didn't. She stayed calm and unbothered as if nothing had happened. And then she said words that made me sick.

"Mothers do that sometimes. You will understand when you have children. Now let's go shopping."

So, we went shopping. Like nothing had happened. And do you know what I told her that day? The words still cut me open when I think about them.

"Mother, even if you dragged me by my hair from one side of the bridge to the other, even if you hurt me, you're still my mother, and I'll still love you."

I can still see the grin that spread across her face. It wasn't a mother's smile, it was a victory. She loved hearing those words.

Back then, I didn't understand. I thought that was what love was supposed to look like: no matter what she did, I owed her devotion.

I thought loyalty meant worshipping even the hands that hurt me.

Now, I look back and see a girl who had no awareness, no tools, no way to know that love isn't supposed to humiliate. That love doesn't slap you into a wall in front of strangers and then take you shopping like nothing happened.

But at that time, I couldn't see it. I was blinded. And she never let me forget it. She still reminds me of those words as if they were her greatest prize.

She twisted my love into her weapon and used it against me.

"HEALING DOESN'T MEAN ERASING THE PAST. IT MEANS REFUSING TO LET IT OWN THE REST OF YOUR LIFE.
THE MOMENT YOU STOP WAITING FOR THE SINCERE APOLOGY THAT WILL NEVER COME, YOU START TO HEAL."

Lina Langford

She Always Knew What She Was Doing

Years passed. I was almost 27 years old. I moved far away from her. New country. New life. A fresh start. I learned fast you can run away from a place, not from what happened there.

I got married. Found a job. Tried to build a normal life. But my first marriage didn't even make it two years. He lied to me from the beginning. Told me he was in law school and almost graduating. After we got married, I found out he quit in his last year. He wasn't going to be a lawyer.

One day we were arguing and he pushed me down the stairs. I remember the shock more than the fall. I grabbed my bag and went to a hotel, scared and shaking.

The next day, I was at work pretending my life wasn't falling apart. Then police officers showed up. He had put a restraining order on me. He told them that I was the abusive one. He was four times bigger than me. Even the officer didn't believe him, but he still had to serve the paper.

I was terrified. Everywhere I went, I thought I saw him. Someone with his walk. His smile. His stare. I didn't feel safe anywhere.

To make things worse, sometimes my mother would visit me. Nothing changed with her.
Same fights. Same drama.

Her trying to open the car door while I was driving. Insulting me and yelling in my house like she owned it. I felt embarrassed in front of my neighbors...again.

I was exhausted.

Tired of fear.

Tired of pretending.

Tired of feeling alone even when I wasn't.

One day, I just drove. I didn't care where. Toward the mountains. I cried and pleaded with God the entire way. "Please...send me my soulmate. Someone who won't hurt me."

I wasn't asking for a miracle. I was asking for peace. And somehow God heard me.

Not long after, I met my husband. The one who was my safe place, I knew it the moment he looked at me. He was calm, very kind, hard working and loving.

Good to the core.

We started a life together. I got pregnant, and we were over the moon.

I had some complications when I was pregnant with my daughter. I ended up in the hospital for almost three months. It was a scary time. I didn't know what was going to happen or if my baby was going to be okay.

And it's strange, but it was the first time in my life I saw my mother look worried about me. She even came to the hospital to take care of me. She was really worried.

I didn't understand it then. I didn't know how to process it. I wasn't used to seeing her this concerned about me.

When she looked at the ultrasound image, she immediately said my daughter looked like her. She was convinced. She asked everyone around if they agreed with her. It mattered to her in a way I couldn't explain back then.

It was confusing. On one side, she showed a tiny piece of care. On the other side, she made it about herself even before my daughter was born. She even chose what career she would have and how her personality would be.

It's like she needed proof that this new life somehow belonged to her story, not mine.

And I think that was the moment I realized even when she seemed loving there was always something underneath it.

Her control. Her ownership. Her big ego.

Even during one of the most vulnerable times of my life, she still found a way to make it about her.

Our daughter came along. She was so precious and most importantly she was healthy.

One day, we were visiting one of my mother's friends. I was nursing my daughter, holding her tiny body in my arms, when the conversation turned once again.

My mother began to complain about me again. She complained about the way I changed diapers, the way I breastfed. She painted herself as patient, as wise, as the loving mother she had never been. She loved being the victim. That was her favorite role.

Then the subject of violence against children came up.

I couldn't stay silent. I turned to her and said, "How can you pretend? How can you forget all those beatings?"

She didn't flinch. Her face hardened, her eyes turned cruel, and she said, "I'm glad I did. You deserved every single one of them."

Most of the time, all these years, she pretended she didn't remember. She would say I was overreacting since I was a child or that I was making a big deal out of nothing. Maybe she spanked me here and there, but real beatings? Those were my exaggerations.

But that day, I knew she remembered every single one. I could see it in her eyes and hear it in her words.

Her words pierced me deeper than any fist. That night, I couldn't breastfeed my daughter. For three days, my milk dried up from the sadness that consumed me. Fever took over my body and I had to feed my baby formula instead.

Because even as a grown woman, even as a mother myself, her cruelty still had the power to wound me.

A Life Spent Trying to Please

My life was not my own. It was sacrificed to please her.

From the moment I could remember, every step, every word, every choice was about whether my mother would be satisfied. Her moods ruled the air we breathed. If she smiled, the day felt safe. If her eyes turned dark, everyone scattered like frightened animals. I learned early that my survival depended on keeping her happy, and yet no matter how much I gave she was never satisfied.

When I first married, especially after my daughter was born, a strange thing happened inside me. I would sit by the crib, run my fingers through my baby's soft hair, and whisper promises to her. Promises that I would never hurt her, never curse her, never break her the way I was broken. But as I sat there, filled with love for my child, I kept asking myself one question over and over. *How could my mother do what she did to me?*

I didn't have an answer.

Awareness came slowly, like waking up from a long sleep. It was painful. I thought I was strong, but the truth was I was still trapped. I didn't know where to put my strength, or how to aim it. My only target was still her. All I wanted, even as a married woman, even as a mother, was to make my mother happy.

One day with that sharp, cutting tone of hers, she looked at me and said, "You've changed."

"How come?" I asked.

Her reply was cold. "Because now your first priority is your husband and your child. It should always be me first. Then your children. Then your husband."

She said it as if it were the natural order of the world. As if it were a universal truth that mothers should come before the families their daughters build. She said it with no shame, no hesitation, no awareness of how sick it sounded.

And for a while, I almost believed her.

But years later, in a therapy session, I finally told her the words I had carried in my chest for decades. "I will never be a mother like you. I am raising my children the opposite way."

She didn't cry. She didn't apologize. She didn't soften.

She smirked.

"Ungrateful," she said. And then the knife twisted even more. "You owe everything to me. Every bit of what you have exists because of me."

That was the truth of her love. It wasn't love at all. It was a bill. A lifelong invoice she shoved into my hands every time I tried to stand on my own.

My past wasn't about me. It was about her. My childhood, my marriage, my motherhood all of it bent to her shadow. My life was a tribute I never agreed to pay.

However, she never took ownership of my mistakes. They belonged to me and me alone.

Yes, of course I made mistakes. Many of them. And I paid the price, over and over again.

Every single one of them was thrown back at me by my mother, by my brother, by my stepfather. They never let me forget. All those mistakes, all those years, as if they themselves were spotless. As if they were perfectly fine.

Even now, after all these years, when we sit together, they still dredge up my past. They laugh at it. They call it a *joke*. And when I try to defend myself, when I finally speak, they twist it back on me again and blame me.

"You just can't handle a joke."

But here's the truth: I learned from my mistakes. I may not be proud of them but each one taught me something. Each one made me stronger.

But slowly, piece by piece, I started to see: my life does not belong to her. My children do not belong to her. My joy does not belong to her.

And I swore, I will never pass that curse down.

Her Golden Ticket

We had some days where we laughed, too. But not many. And even those moments, the few that slipped through, never lasted. They always ended the same way; with yelling, with insults, with her dragging the fun into the mud. I could feel myself firing back sometimes, because how much can one person hold in? But the second I pushed back, the whole thing went up in flames. That's how it always was. Any magic we managed to find burned out fast.

One day she came to me with what she called her brilliant idea. A sneaky idea, really. She told me she had hired a family therapist and said all of us- me, my stepfather, my brother, and her were going to therapy. She looked right at me, her face full of fake concern, and asked, "Would you join us?"

Of course, I said yes. In fact, I had begged for something like that for years. I wanted it more than anything. Maybe this was finally the chance to fix what was broken. Maybe we could heal.

The beatings had stopped long ago, but the emotional abuse hadn't. If therapy could help us speak honestly, if it could calm the storm, then yes, sign me up.

But soon the truth hit me like a brick. A few months in, I realized I was sitting there alone. Alone in family therapy.

Every time I asked the therapist how things were going with my brother, she sighed and told me he was too busy. When I asked about my stepfather, she said he wasn't allowed to speak without my mother right next to him. So it was just me on those zoom calls.

Just me.

My mother had painted this picture of all of us working through things together, but she knew from the start it wouldn't last. It was always just going to be me.

I remember one Zoom call in particular. The therapist asked me to open up, to tell my mother how I felt. So, I did. I poured everything out, the hurt, the pain, the years of destruction. And my mother sat there, stone faced. Not a flicker of sad emotion. Sometimes, when I said something raw, something that should've cut her to the core, she smirked. A snarky smile while I was hurting. She had no shame.

None.

Before therapy and my newfound awareness, I was a fireball. All those years of abuse had left me angry, restless, confused. I didn't understand what was happening inside me, didn't understand her twisted mind, her narcissism, her disorder, whatever it was. I couldn't diagnose it, but I lived through it. And she knew exactly what she was doing when she chose that therapist.

The woman was inexperienced. Too soft. Too easy to play. My mother thought she could fool her, twist her, convince her that I was the problem, that I was unstable.

And the truth is, I probably looked unstable, mad and fired up back then. I was angry, raw and quick to blow. And my mother calmly sat there, letting me look like the crazy one. That was her golden ticket.

Then the lies started spreading. She told my aunt that the therapist had said I was mentally sick. She told my brother the same thing. She told my stepfather, too. Friends. Neighbors. Anyone who would listen. And suddenly it wasn't her saying it anymore, it was the "therapist's diagnosis."

I couldn't believe it. That wasn't true. Not even close.

The therapist actually told me something completely different. She said yes, I was angry in the beginning, but I was changing. She was very proud of me, but I chose to focus on myself, not on her. She even recommended books on self-discovery and awareness. That was the truth.

But my mother didn't need the truth. She just needed one tiny crack she could twist.

And just like that, I became the "mentally sick daughter."

That was her new story, and they listened. Of course they did. Because if they didn't, she would make their lives hell. She wasn't the easy one, they knew that.

So, they obeyed her.

And me? Who was I? Just the sick girl, right?

When I found out, my world turned upside down. I lost it. I called the therapist, screaming, crying, completely out of my mind.

"How could you say that? How could you let her tell people this?"

The therapist swore she never did. She told me my mother had twisted her words from the very beginning. She reminded me of what she had actually said, that I was angry but I was changing. That I was growing into a better version of myself. She told me the only way out was to stay away and protect myself from all her games. And she said that would only come with awareness.

But it didn't matter at that moment. The damage was already done. My mother had her story and she used it like a weapon once again.

Not long after, I woke up one morning and felt something shift in me. I can't explain it, but I knew I wasn't the same as yesterday.

Something cracked open inside.

And I told myself, *I'm not going back. I'm not the same person anymore. I could feel it.*

It wasn't an easy path. After her sneaky family therapist plan I never looked at her the same way. I developed severe panic attacks. Panic attacks feel like the end of the world when they come. I will never forget the first one I ever had.

We were on the highway. My chest tightened. My vision blurred. I couldn't breathe. My heart was about to explode. I was sure I was dying. My husband pulled over, his hands shaking as he dialed 911. My children sat in the backseat, my daughter with her eyes wide, my little boy too young to understand but sensing something was wrong.

I thought I'd never see them again.

My husband kept trying to help me breathe, his voice steady even though I could hear the fear in it.

That moment felt endless. It changed me. It shaped me differently. And if it weren't for my husband, I truly believe I might have had a heart attack that day.

Panic attacks don't have to own you forever.

Over the next two years, I rebuilt myself. Slowly. Messily. But I did it. I went to hypnosis sessions. I took breathing lessons. I read more books than I can count and listened to endless podcasts about healing, trauma, and nervous system regulation. I tried everything. I still feel it sometimes, but thankfully not as severely as before.

I went all the way to Montana for healing therapy with horses, trying to find myself. My healing got somewhat easier after my therapy in Montana. That experience changed my life. Her name was Donna, a beautiful, strong therapy horse. When I was with her, she would roll on the ground next to me, rub her head against me, almost like she was taking my pain away. There are no words for what it felt like. That horse gave me a kind of comfort I didn't even know I was still searching for.

Today, I can manage my panic attacks. They don't control me anymore. But I still think of Donna often. I plan to go back one day soon, not because I need to but because I want to thank her in person.

Healing isn't a straight line. It's a long, messy road filled with small victories. But if you're reading this and struggling, please know that you're not alone. Panic attacks don't have to be the end of your story. They can be the start of your healing.

At the beginning of my healing process I cut all contact. For two years, I disappeared. And then, after two years of silence, she came back with her fake sweetness. Fake smile.

"My baby girl. My princess. My sweetheart."

Forty six years of life, she had never called me those words.

And suddenly I was a princess?

Suddenly, I was her baby girl, especially when someone was around.

I almost laughed. I should've handed her a crown for the performance.

She plays her games differently now. Not with fists, but with words. Not with bruises, but with strategy. She calls me sweet names that make my stomach turn upside down. She thinks she's winning me back with "love."

But it's not love.

It's the same poison, just poured into a prettier cup.

And the more she calls me those fake names, the more I feel sick.

Because I know. I've always known.

And now, finally, I can't unsee it.

YOU COULD HAVE FORGIVEN, IF THERE HAD BEEN TRUTH IN THEIR APOLOGY. FORGIVENESS IS POSSIBLE ONLY WHEN THERE'S REMORSE.BUT WHEN YOU SEE THEIR EVIL ACTIONS HAVE NO LIMITS,FORGIVENESS BECOMES SELF-BETRAYAL."

Lina Langford

Locked Hands

Let me take you back to one of my childhood memories. There are nights that never leave you, no matter how many years pass. Some memories blur at the edges, but others stay sharp, like glass you can't spit out.

One of those nights, I was shattered. My mother left us with my grandparents so she could marry her fiancé. She wasn't just moving to another town or another city. She was moving to another country, thousands of miles away.

The night before she left, I asked her, "Mom, this is your last night. Can we sleep together?"

Her answer cut deep. "I can't sleep if someone is touching me. Go to your bed. I can't sleep with someone."

Then she left the next day.

But since that day, she has never once slept alone. She never remembers saying those words. She never admits them.

I know I chose the wrong friends, but my brother got mixed up with people who were far more dangerous.

She used to send money, but Grandpa rarely shared it. He said it would spoil us. I told Mom what he was doing. Maybe in his mind he was saving for us, but I had no way of knowing that.

Her response on the phone crushed me. "I'm done with you guys. I've started my own path without you guys." *And she hung up.*

I dropped to the floor, my body curling in on itself. My hands clenched so hard my nails pierced my skin. My feet locked tight, like my whole body wanted to disappear.

And that's when my little brother walked in.

He froze. His eyes widened when he saw me twisted on the ground. Then he rushed over, small hands tugging at mine, trying to pry my fingers open.

"Sister," he whispered. *Sister.* "Open your hands, sister. Please, open your hands."

That word – *sister* - sank deep inside me. It was the sweetest thing I had ever heard. My whole body ached, but hearing my brother call me that filled me with a strange comfort. For once, someone saw me. Someone cared.

And so I squeezed tighter. The more he tried to open my hands, the tighter I locked them, because I didn't want him to stop.

I wanted him to stay there with me, to keep calling me sister, to keep caring. I wanted him to love me enough to keep trying.

That moment carved something dangerous into me: attention could come from pain. Care could be pulled from suffering. If I hurt enough, maybe someone would finally see me.

I locked my body like that more than once, at least three times. And every time, my brother would panic and try to save me.

The attention felt like love. And in a home where real love didn't exist, I clung to anything that resembled it.

Until one day, I ended up in a hospital bed. The doctor told my brother my body was seizing itself from psychological trauma. To them, I was just a difficult, dramatic girl. To me, I was drowning in pain no one else could see.

I promised myself then: never again. I would never chase care through suffering. I would never let my body become a prison for attention.

But life is cruel.

Years later, my brother brought it up to me. His voice wasn't tender that time. He didn't remember the fear in his eyes or the way he whispered *sister*. He remembered it as evidence.

"Remember, you couldn't even open your hands," he said. As if that proved my mother was right. As if my suffering was a weakness that belonged to me, not to her cruelty.

That day, something in me closed. Whatever was left of a bond between us as siblings ended. Because how could I ever call him brother again when he used my pain as proof that I was the problem?

The truth is, he never really called me *sister* again. My name was *girl*. That's how he always called me.

Not with love, not with meaning.

A handful of times in our entire lives he called me *sister* and two of those were on the nights my hands were locked, my body trembling, my heart desperate for care.

He stopped being my brother the day he chose her story over mine.

Once again, bribery won.

Now that's why I'm extremely careful when raising our children, teaching them how to love, respect, and protect each other. When I see my son showing so much love for his sister, it touches my heart in a special way. It's not just a reminder that I'm nothing like my mother, but also that he loves his sister the way I always wished my brother had loved me.

The Ritual of Fairness

You might laugh if you saw me in my kitchen today.

The way I cut apples. The way I measure chicken on a plate. The way I portion soup.

Every time I serve food to my children, I check and double check to make sure it's equal. If one apple slice looks slightly bigger than the other, I trim it down. If one piece of meat is heavier, I shift little bites until the plates look the same. Not because my children ever demand it but because I remember what it feels like to live in a house where love was given in crumbs.

I will not let my children ever wonder if one of them is loved more.

My mother used affection as a weapon. She turned care into performance. She praised only when it could make her look good to others. And when she was cruel, she was merciless. I grew up believing love had to be earned, and still, even when you gave everything, it was never enough.

That's why I obsess over fairness. For me, it isn't about the apple. It isn't about the chicken. It's about undoing what was done to me. It's about showing my children that love is not conditional, not measured, not handed out to the child who pleases me the most.

Love in my home is abundant.

It overflows.

So yes, I cut apples with precision. I weigh soup with my eyes. I hug my children until they can't breathe. I kiss their hair, their cheeks, their hands. I tell them every day over and over, "You are loved. You are enough. You don't have to earn it."

Because I know what it feels like to grow up starving for something you should have been given freely.

And I refuse to pass that starvation down.

What I Can't Unsee

Remember, when I was little, I used to sit in the pasture across from my grandparents' house, drawing pictures in the dirt? I'd sketch a small house, a roof, and inside it, a boy and a girl. My children. I'd whisper to God: *I promise. I'll never hurt them. Just give me a chance to build a home filled with love.*

That promise has been the spine of my life.

I will never forget the words she used against me, spoken so many times with a twisted joy in her eyes, spit flying from her mouth as she begged God to make those curses come true.

"I wish I'd given birth to a stone instead of you...May every drop of milk I ever gave be poison to you. May it rise up in you and make you suffer for the rest of your life...I hope God gives you a child just like you. May life make you suffer the way you made me suffer."

I used to wonder what I could have possibly done to deserve those curses

I grew up believing that maybe I was the problem.

Those words, those curses, those humiliations.

I cannot unsee them.

I cannot unknow them.

They are burned into me.

I cannot forget.

How can you call yourself a good person when your words cut deeper than any blade, when they drip worse than poison?

How can you stand there, looking like the devil, and pretend you're clean?

Turn around and say, *"My tongue is sharp, but my heart is clean."* What kind of lie is that?

A clean heart doesn't spit curses on its own child.

A clean heart doesn't pray for her own child's suffering, year after year without pause. If your mouth is a weapon, if your words are a curse, then your heart is no different.

If her heart were truly clean, she would admit what she's done. She would apologize and ask her daughter for sincere forgiveness, not try to convince others that her daughter, who has two precious children and a wonderful husband, was mentally ill.

Instead, she said, *"Am I supposed to apologize to the shit I pooped out?"*

I was no different than shit to her, and she had no mercy saying that. Not just to me over and over to my face only, but she told others, too.

When I put myself in her place and think of saying something like that to my own daughter, subjecting her to that type of abuse, I feel like I am losing my mind.

But here is the truth:

Because I cannot unsee them, I will not repeat them.

Because I cannot unknow them, I can choose differently.

Because I lived them, my children never will.

My home is not a balance sheet.

My love is not a debt. My hands are not weapons.
My children will never doubt if they are loved, wanted, cherished.

This is what survival looks like.

Not just being alive after the fire but building a home in the ashes where love finally lives.

The only real weapon my mother ever had, the only true power, was the money that came through my stepfather. And once I became a young woman, she used it in every way she could.

My stepfather became an atheist years ago. His choices are not my business but the reason always struck me as interesting.

His reason?

He told me, *"If God was real, He wouldn't let children be born crippled."*

But he couldn't see the child in front of him being broken down with emotional violence all these years. He turned his head away, defended his wife just to keep his peace, just to keep me from disrupting his comfort. He refused to see what became of me. But he could abandon his faith over some excuse, some so-called reason close to home. He told me many times that if he said something, she would disturb his comfort. So, he acted like he never saw or heard anything all these years. He admitted that to me. He even asked me to keep quiet, to not respond when she insulted me or lied because he lives with her and he pays the price with his peace.

Yet he is mad at God for letting children suffer.

"HEALING STARTS AT ROCK BOTTOM. YOU EITHER DROWN...OR RISE. THE CHOICE IS YOURS."

Lina Langford

The Golden Child

I remember asking her once what her priorities were. Who were the most important people in her life? Without even thinking, she said, "Myself first. Always myself. And then my husband. When I get old, he will take care of me."

Me and my brother weren't even on her list back then. We didn't even cross her mind.

And yet, years later here we are now. She must have added him to her list by now, because at forty-five years old, my brother still hasn't worked in over twelve years. And somehow, he always has money to enjoy life comfortably.

He lives in their house. Free life. Full shelter. A car with a full tank of gas. Bills paid. Vacations. Restaurants. Financial support for every one of his so-called brilliant business ideas. Ideas that always ended up in disaster, money swallowed up like a black hole.

And me? Yes, they helped me through the years here and there, filling holes when the cries got too loud. But never the full comfort. Never the stability. Never the free ride like he has. They never gave me the life they gave him. Not that I'd even want to live the way he does, but it hurts.

Yes, I still love my brother. But I hate that she built this wall between us, that she created this game where bribery wins, but love never does.

I was working hard, still ending up desperate sometimes. One day I asked if they could give me the same comfort they had given him all these years. I wasn't asking to be spoiled. I was asking for relief. For help. The same way they are providing for my brother.

They said no.

They told me to sell some of my clothes and pay my bills. That I should've been more careful.

Of course, they are not obligated to do anything. But it still hurt when they rubbed it in my face, poked me in the eye and then turned around to give me advice. *You should've been more careful. Sell your clothes if you can't pay your bills.*

Six months after I asked that, she video called me. Her voice was light, almost cheerful. She pointed at my brother, smiling, and said,

"Things will be better soon. He has something in mind."

I almost laughed, but I didn't. I already knew. He always had some idea, some dream that was nothing more than smoke. And I always warned them. I told them he was being scammed. I told them over and over. They didn't listen.

Instead, they turned that back on me. They told me I was jealous. In their mind that's why I couldn't stand him trying to be successful.

And then, like clockwork, it all went wrong. Another business gone. Another disaster. Another hole. And they still refused to see it.

That day, after telling me about his new idea, she looked at me. She smiled, almost tender, and said, "Don't worry, baby. I prayed for you."

If you've ever wondered what evil dressed up as comfort looks like, this is it.

That fake softness.

That empty blessing.

That insult that feels holy on the outside but cuts like poison on the inside.

Money was always presented as love. If we received it, it meant we were "good." If we didn't, it was punishment, proof that we weren't loved. Maybe that's why money became my weakness.

I crave stability.

That was the system. That was the game.

Almost half a century, it sounds easy to say but to live life the way I did, it shapes you. It's not easy to question everything when this is all you've ever known.

And even after everything, after all the damage, I still have to watch them enjoy themselves, rubbing it in my face, turning two siblings into enemies. And I'll admit, sometimes that hurts more.

They always think they're teaching me a lesson when they abandon me, just so they can rub it in my face later. My mother taught them well.

This is why I act paranoid when I cut apples or serve food for my children, making sure every piece is the same, every portion fair. Because I know what it feels like to grow up believing love can be uneven.

Of course, my brother and I are different. He is the golden child. But I still love him. He never liked to work, still doesn't. He's always had these "brilliant ideas," but it's always someone else's fault that things didn't work out.

It's never his mistake. Just bad luck.

Always bad luck.

And me? I kept working. With a drive inside me that never seems to die. Not to prove anything to anyone, but because it has become who I am. My identity. My way of being.

I can't even imagine sitting around waiting for life to hand me something. The thought of it makes me miserable. That's not me.

But still, it's painful to watch. To see them choose to press harder, to hurt me on purpose. To rub the knife in.

At some point though, you just let go.

You leave it behind so fully, so deeply, that all that's left to say is...

Fuck it.

And when you say it, truly, from the bottom of your heart, so much else goes with it. The weight, the memories, the chains. They all begin to fade.

You can't stop it!

Maybe I was waiting for justice. Perhaps fairness. Just to see if, even once in my life, they could love me the way they loved my brother. But that day never came. And deep down, I think I always knew it never would. Because in their eyes, I was already painted as the jealous sister, the one who could never measure up to the golden child.

The End of the Inheritance

This is the part where most people expect forgiveness. They expect a neat ending, a ribbon tied over decades of bruises and silence.

They expect me to say, *"But she was still my mother, and I forgave her."*

But that is not my ending.

Forgiveness is not the gift I owe her. Survival is the gift I gave myself. And breaking the cycle is the gift I give my children.

I don't hate her and I don't wish on her the things she wished on me my entire life. But I don't see her the same way anymore.

I just can't unsee it.

My story was never about becoming her mirror. It was about refusing to carry her reflection forward.

It was about taking the curses spoken over me- *bitch, slut, ungrateful, mistake, unworthy, shit-* and burning them in a fire so they would never pass through my lips to the ears of my children.

When my mother looked at me and repeatedly said she wished she would have given birth to a stone instead of me, she was trying to kill something in me. And for a long time, she almost did.

But she forgot one thing, stones don't die. Stones endure.

Stones weather storms and hold their place.

Maybe she was right without knowing it.

Maybe I was the stone.

But I was not cold or lifeless. I was a stone carved by God's own hand, shaped to endure what should have broken me, and strong enough to build a foundation my children can stand on.

My grandparents are not alive anymore. They both passed away. I didn't inherit anything financially other than a couple of their personal items as memories that I will cherish forever.

But they left me something *much* bigger.

They taught me how to be *grateful*.

They taught me how to have *principles* in my life, how to *love* the right way, how to *respect* others.

They taught me how to keep my *ego* in balance.

I look at my husband, my children, my home, and I see proof.

Proof that love can exist without cruelty.

Proof that a family can be safe, not suffocating. Proof that a woman raised on curses can grow into a mother who blesses every breath her children take.

I was buried again and again.

But I clawed my way up through the dirt and I planted myself in the light.

I have some memories I still keep locked inside. They are too painful to share right now, wounds that still burn when touched. Maybe one day I will be ready.

This book is not about sadness.

It is about thriving.

About survival.

About choosing to live free when every chain has been placed on you.

And if you carry nothing else from my story, carry this:

You are not what they called you.

You are not the curses spoken over you.

You are not the bruise, the silence, or the locked door.

You are the one who decides where the cycle ends.

And when you decide, you will be free.